Welcome to Israel!

by Lilly Rivlin with Gila Gevirtz

Editorial Committee

Rabbi Morrison D. Bial

Dr. Itzik Eshel

Dr. Robert O. Freedman

Yossef Lando

Chani Oppenheim

Okay, you can turn to the next page—I'll catch up to you soon!

BEHRMAN HOUSE, INC.

Project Manager:
Gila Gevirtz

Developmental Editor:
Hara Person

Assistant Editor:
Alison Minion

Designer:
Pronto Design
& Production, Inc.

To Tzvi, Ronni, Lance, and Michelle, and to their children. May you all come to love Israel.

—LR

And to Michael: "Bind me as a seal upon your heart, a sign upon your hand" (The Song of Songs 8:6).

—GG

The publisher gratefully acknowledges the assistance of: Yigal Rechtman, Elana Rechtman, Ora Baumgarten, Yigal Baumgarten, Rabbi Arik Ascherman, and the children of Kibbutz Tzora.

Manufactured in the United States of America

Library of Congress Cataloging-in-Publication Data

Rivlin, Lilly.

    Welcome to Israel / by Lilly Rivlin with Gila Gevirtz.

        p. cm.

        Summary: Illustrations, photographs, maps, and text introduce the history, culture, religions, and peoples of Israel.

            ISBN 0-87441-692-2

        1. Israel—Juvenile literature. [1. Israel.] I. Gevirtz, Gila. II. Title.

DS118 .R57 2000

956.94—dc21

                                        00-021713

Contents

ARTISTS

JoAnn Adinolfi, illustrations; Donna Ingemanson, borders; Chris Renaud, maps

PHOTO CREDITS

Agence France Presse/Corbis: 34; Alex Archer Photography: 73; American Technion Society: 63 (bottom); Consulate General of Israel in New York: 27 (bottom), 109, 120, 123 (top); Creative Image: 7; El Al Airlines: cover (left of center), 32 (top); Gila Gevirtz: cover (lower left), 20, 23 (top), 37 (top), 41 (bottom), 46, 56 (bottom), 57 (bottom), 58, 101 (bottom), 104 (bottom), 118; Hadassah: The Women's Zionist Organization of America: 13, 109; Israeli Scouts: cover (upper right), 98; Israel Ministry of Tourism: cover (center, center bottom, and lower right), 33, 44 (bottom), 51, 53, 56–57 (top), 60, 61, 63 (top), 67, 69, 70, 72, 74–79, 81, 104 (top), 107, 113 (bottom); Israel Office of Information: 19 (coins); Jewish National Fund: 83; Francene Keery: 19 (bottom); Richard Lobell: 6, 15 (bottom), 27 (top), 28, 29, 32 (bottom), 40, 54, 59, 63, 64, 84, 90 (top), 91, 97, 123 (bottom), 124; Hara Person: 23 (middle), 27 (middle), 45, 47, 90 (bottom), 99, 100, 101 (top), 102 (top), 105, 110; Vittoriano Rastelli/Corbis: 116; David Rubinger/Corbis: 121; Oskar Tauber: 111; Zionist Archives and Library: 12, 108, 113 (top).

Hi! You don't know me, yet—but you will soon. I need a favor. Please fill in the blanks on this page so that I have a complete map of Israel. Don't worry, you'll get the help you need to do it as you read this book.

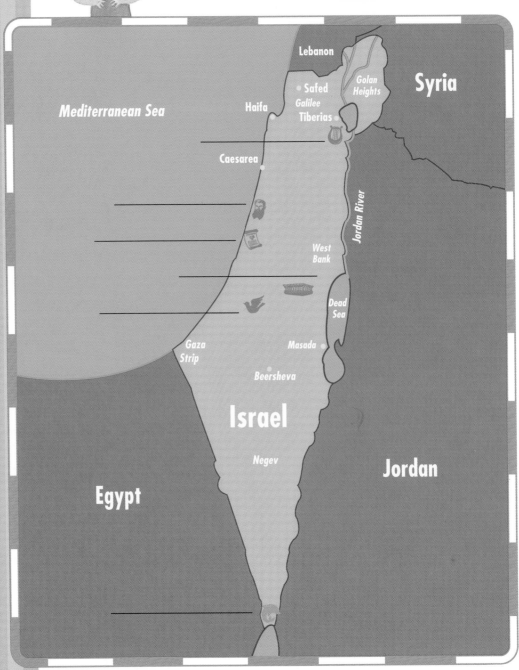

Lebanon

Syria

Golan Heights

Safed

Galilee

Haifa

Tiberias

Mediterranean Sea

Caesarea

Jordan River

West Bank

Dead Sea

Masada

Gaza Strip

Beersheva

Israel

Negev

Jordan

Egypt

Welcome

to Our Homeland

Natan

Shalom!
My name is Liat, and I live in Israel. I'm in the fifth grade, and these are some of my friends. Please join us as we learn about our country. We will visit with kids from all over Israel.

The first thing we will do is find out why Israel has played such an important part in the story of the Jewish people. We will also learn how the modern State of Israel came to be.

Let's get started!

Shalom. I'm Liat's kid brother, Natan. Liat is smart and lots of fun, but she can be so bossy and annoying. She calls me "The Nudnik," but I don't let it bother me.

I'm Liat

A Land of Opposites

Israel is a small country—about the size of New Jersey! Yet, for such a small country, Israel is chock-full of opposites.

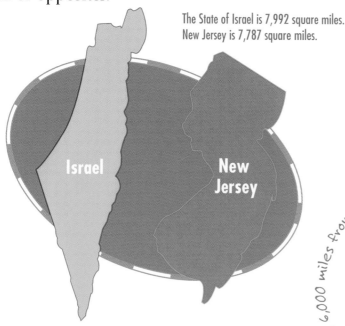

The State of Israel is 7,992 square miles. New Jersey is 7,787 square miles.

It's like flying from New York to Los Angeles and back! That's a long trip. It is 6,000 miles from the United States. Israel is smaller than 41 of the 50 states in the United States.

To begin with, Israel is both very old *and* very new. As we travel around the country, you will see many places that are described in the Bible. So, Israel must be very old. But the modern State of Israel—**Medinat Yisrael**—is filled with airports, highways, video arcades, and fast food restaurants. So, Israel is also very new.

The land itself is full of opposites. The Dead Sea, in eastern Israel, is 1,300 feet *below* sea level. It is the lowest point on earth! Yet, only a few hours drive to the north is Mount Hermon, which has a ski resort. Mount Hermon's snowy peaks rise to over 9,000 feet *above* sea level! Getting chilly? Just drive back south to Eilat, where it is warm enough to go snorkeling, even in the winter.

Look carefully at the keys on this computer keyboard. What do you notice? In Israel, the language of the Bible is also the language of the Internet.

At once very old *and* very new, very low *and* very high, very cold *and* very warm, Israel is full of surprises and full of fun. It is like no other place on earth—and it is just like home no matter where you are from.

Shalom aleichem! Welcome to *Medinat Yisrael!* Welcome to our homeland!

Most of Mount Hermon is in Syria. Only about 7 percent is in Israel. The part of Mount Hermon that is in Israel was captured by Israel in the Six-Day War, in 1967.

Every week in synagogue, we read a portion, or *parashah,* from the Torah. Many of these portions teach us about the importance of *Eretz Yisrael* to the Jewish people.

The Bible: A Family Album

The Bible is like a family album. It tells us the stories of our ancestors who lived almost 4,000 years ago in the Land of Israel—**Eretz Yisrael**. In fact, Israel is often called the Land of the Bible.

In Genesis, the first book of the Torah, we read that Abraham and Sarah were the first Jews. Our tradition teaches that Abraham left the city of Ur (in modern Iraq) to settle in Canaan—which is what *Eretz Yisrael* was called in ancient times—because God told him to do so. The Bible also teaches that God promised the Land of Israel to Abraham as a homeland for his descendants.

Did you know that when you say "Medinat Yisrael" and "Eretz Yisrael," you are speaking Ivrit—Hebrew!

7

Abraham and Sarah were not only the first Jews, they were the first Jews to live in the Land of Israel. But they weren't the first to be *born* there. That honor goes to their son. Do you know his name?

Isaac

After a few generations, famine forced the Israelites—the ancient Jews—to go down to Egypt where there was food. At first life was good there, but then a new pharaoh, or king, arose and enslaved the Israelites. The Bible teaches that God heard the Israelites' cries and sent Moses to lead them out of Egypt. Moses led the Israelites out of Egypt, but died before reaching the Land of Israel. Joshua, the next leader, brought our ancestors into Israel.

Olive trees are plentiful in Israel. In biblical times olive oil was used not only for eating, but also for anointing kings and as fuel for the menorah in the Holy Temple. The Syrians who ruled ancient Israel destroyed all but a small amount of the Temple's supply of olive oil. Miraculously, the remaining oil lasted for eight days, until a fresh supply was available. Which Jewish holiday celebrates this miracle?

When the ancient Babylonians conquered Israel in 586 BCE (more than 2,500 years ago), our ancestors were forced to leave the land. While some settled in Babylonia, others went to Egypt, Yemen, Persia, and beyond. This was the beginning of the Diaspora, the Jewish communities living outside of Israel.

Jews were permitted to return to the Land of Israel in 538 BCE by Cyrus, the king of Persia. Jerusalem was rebuilt and the Second Temple was constructed. Then, in the second century BCE, the Second Temple was taken over by the Syrians who followed the Greek ways—dressing in Greek robes, speaking the Greek language, reading Greek books, and playing Greek sports. The Syrians put Greek idols in the Second Temple.

Did You Know?

There is no remnant of the First Temple except for an ivory staff, or rod, used by a *kohen*, a Temple priest, of the time. The staff is exhibited in the Israel Museum in Jerusalem.

I made it! I knew Liat wanted to leave without me but I can't miss this—there's so much to see and do.

Under Judah the Maccabee, the Jews drove out the Syrians in 165 BCE and rededicated the Temple to God, establishing our holiday of Ḥanukkah. Later, King Herod completely rebuilt the Second Temple so that it was greater and more beautiful than ever. But when the Romans conquered Israel and destroyed the Temple in 70 CE, many of our ancestors were again forced from the land. This time, our people spread out over the entire world. Eventually, almost all the Jews were driven out of Israel, but we prayed that one day we would return.

Birth of a Nation

Beginning in the 1500s, Jews in many European countries were forced to live separately from other peoples in sections of the cities called ghettos. The Jews lived in poverty and without basic freedoms. Laws limited where Jews could shop and travel, with whom they could visit and do business, and the type of work they could do. Many Jews were killed in riots inspired by anti-Semitism—prejudice against Jews—and their property was taken or destroyed.

Stones from the Western Wall

In the late 1800s, Theodor Herzl, a Hungarian-born Jewish writer and journalist, became enraged by the treatment of European Jews. He believed that the Jews must have a homeland of their own and that they should reclaim Zion, the Land of Israel.

In 1897, Herzl organized the First Zionist Congress, which brought together Jewish leaders from around the world. He was elected president of the newly created World Zionist Organization. Herzl dedicated the rest of his life to Zionism—the commitment to creating and supporting an independent Jewish state in *Eretz Yisrael.*

As the popularity of the Zionist movement grew, thousands of Jews from Russia, Poland, and Germany came to the Land of Israel, which was then called Palestine. These early pioneers, or **ḥalutzim**, left their homes to build new lives in a faraway land that was filled with swamps and malarial disease. They wanted to build a nation that would prosper and live peacefully with its neighbors.

Theodor Herzl (1860–1904) was the father of the Zionist movement. He coined its slogan: "If you will it, it is no dream." Barely 50 years after the First Zionist Congress, Herzl's dream became reality.

Can you imagine leaving your family and friends, and the only home you've ever known, to settle in a new land thousands of miles away? Why do you think the ḥalutzim were so determined to build the Land of Israel?

_____

_____

_____

Israel and Its Neighbors

Map It Out

Many places in Israel are named after Theodor Herzl. Two such places are Mount Herzl and Herzliya. Mount Herzl, in Jerusalem, is the site of a military cemetery where Israel's war heroes and great leaders—including Theodor Herzl and former prime minister Yitzḥak Rabin—are buried. Herzliya is a town on Israel's seacoast.

Turn to the map on page 4 and label Herzliya by writing its name next to Herzl's picture. Name the large body of water off the coast of Herzliya.

_____

On November 29, 1947, the United Nations voted to divide Palestine into three parts. One part was to be under Jewish control, another under Arab control, and the third part—made up of Jerusalem and Bethlehem—was to become an international zone. The Zionists agreed to the plan, but the Arabs rejected it.

The modern State of Israel, *Medinat Yisrael*, was established on May 14, 1948. Jews all around the world celebrated. The European Jewish population had been largely destroyed by the Holocaust, but the birth of the State of Israel offered new hope. After almost 2,000 years without a country, we finally had our homeland again.

When the partitioning, or dividing, of Palestine was announced, Jews celebrated in the streets in cities throughout *Eretz Yisrael*.

The next day, May 15, 1948, armies from the five neighboring Arab countries attacked Israel. Though a young and struggling nation with limited military equipment and numbers of soldiers, Israel won its War of Independence. An armistice was finally signed in 1949 on the Greek island of Rhodes.

Israel has been plagued with many other wars—the Suez War, also called the Sinai Campaign (1956); the Six-Day War (1967); the War of Attrition (1969–1970); the Yom Kippur War (1973); the war in Lebanon (1982–1985); the Intifada (1987–1993); and the Gulf War (1991). Today, Israel is at peace with some of its neighbors, and it continues to work toward peace with others.

Students from 70 developing countries, including Guatemala, the Dominican Republic, the Philippines, Kenya, and Liberia, have graduated from the Hadassah-Hebrew University international public health program. The Israeli government has funded each student with a grant of $24,000!

This program is just one example of Israel's commitment to fighting world hunger, poverty, and disease.

This is the Hadassah-Hebrew University Medical Center in Ein Kerem, Jerusalem.

Henrietta Szold, Hadassah's Heroine

Baltimore-born Henrietta Szold (1860–1945) was a strong and determined person. She was the first woman to study the Talmud and other holy texts at the Jewish Theological Seminary in New York. In 1909, she made her first visit to Palestine. Troubled by the unhealthy living conditions of the children there, Szold returned to New York to form Hadassah, the national organization of Zionist women. For the rest of her life, she worked to improve health care and education in Palestine.

Hadassah Hospital opened in 1925. Today, it has two large hospitals and research laboratories in Jerusalem—one on Mount Scopus and the other in Ein Kerem—and continues to provide quality medical care. The Hadassah Medical Organization has served as a bridge to peace and understanding by treating thousands of Christians and Muslims from neighboring Arab countries.

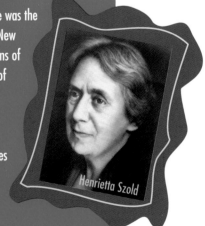

Henrietta Szold

Yom Ha'atzma'ut, Israel's Independence Day, is celebrated on the fifth day of the Jewish month of Iyar. (Iyar usually falls in April or May.) Every year, Israelis celebrate Yom Ha'atzma'ut with parades and picnics. The day before, Yom Hazikaron, Memorial Day, is observed in memory of the soldiers who died defending Israel and the citizens who were killed in terrorist attacks.

On the morning of Yom Hazikaron, sirens blow all across the country, followed by two minutes of complete silence. Throughout Israel, everything stops—talk, traffic, machinery, all activity—as Israelis remember that they owe their freedom to the courage of those whose lives were sacrificed.

When evening comes and the first stars appear, a long siren blast is heard. Yom Hazikaron is over, and Yom Ha'atzma'ut begins. Why do you think these holidays are observed one day after the other?

_____

_____

_____

_____

_____

The Government

Israel is the only real democracy in the Middle East. The prime minister, the head of the government, is elected by the Israeli citizenship. Every citizen 18 and over has the right to vote.

The Israeli parliament is called the Knesset. Its 120 seats are filled by representatives from more than a dozen political parties. The number of representatives from each party is determined by the number of votes each party receives in the national elections.

The president of Israel is elected by the Knesset. Unlike in the United States, where the president is the leader of the government, the role of Israel's president is largely ceremonial. For example, Israel's president may represent the Jewish state at the funeral of an international leader. However, the president does not negotiate treaties with other countries.

← I really had to think about this one.

14

Long before Golda Meir (1898–1978) served as the fourth prime minister of Israel, she was a teacher in Milwaukee, Wisconsin. Born in Russia, Golda Meir immigrated to the United States in 1906 and settled in Eretz Yisrael in 1921.

Matters of law are decided by Israel's Supreme Court. Members of the Supreme Court are appointed by the president on the recommendation of a committee of judges, lawyers, and members of the Knesset. Justices serve until age 70.

Israel's Supreme Court

What Do You Think?

The word *knesset* comes from the same root as *l'hikanes*, meaning "to enter" or "to gather." The Israeli Knesset is a place where elected officials gather to work for the good of the country.

A synagogue is a *beit knesset*—"a house of gathering." When and why do Jews gather in a synagogue?

_____

_____

_____

Map It Out

Turn to the map on page 4 and label Jerusalem by writing its name above the picture of the Knesset. What neighboring country is closest to Jerusalem?

_____

The Knesset is located in Jerusalem, the capital of Israel. Where is your national government located?

Hint:
Think about the times you have come together with other Jews in the synagogue.

National Symbols

Israel's unofficial national anthem is "Hatikvah," which means "The Hope." Long before Israel became independent in 1948, the poem "Hatikvah," written by Naphtali Herz Imber, had become the anthem of the Zionist movement. "Hatikvah" begins:

Within the heart
A Jewish spirit is still alive
And the eyes look eastward
Toward Zion.
Our hope is not lost,
The hope of two thousand years
To be a free nation in our land
In the land of Zion and Jerusalem.

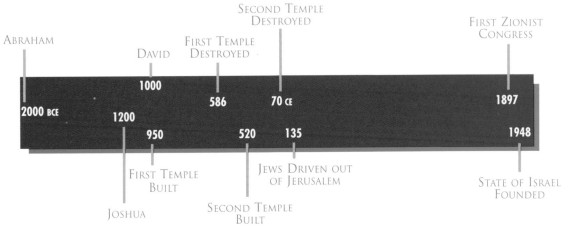

When I have to wait three months for summer vacation or two weeks for my birthday party it feels like forever. Can you imagine what it is like to hope and dream about something for 2,000 years?

What do the words of "Hatikvah" tell you about the Jewish people's continuing love of Israel? How do you think our love of Israel helps Jews around the world—despite the great distances between us— remain as one united community?

The Israeli flag has a white background with two blue stripes, and a blue Magen David—Shield of David, sometimes called a Star of David, or Jewish Star—in the middle. The idea for the flag was based on the tallit, the prayer shawl that Jews wear.

Flags flying across from the Western Wall in Jerusalem

These four Israeli coins, from left to right, are the 1-agorah, 5-, 10-, and 25-agorot coins that replaced the prutah coins in 1960. Can you translate the Hebrew word that appears at the bottom of all four coins?

Israel's state emblem

This coin from *Eretz Yisrael* is 2,000 years old. It is from the time of King Herod.

The menorah is an ancient Jewish symbol, first described in the Bible. The seven-branched menorah is the centerpiece of Israel's official state emblem. The olive branches stretching outward on either side of the menorah represent Israel's yearning for shalom, peace. The ḥanukkiyah we light on Ḥanukkah is very similar to the seven-branched menorah. Describe how the seven-branched menorah and the ḥanukkiyah are different?

_____

_____

_____

Ḥanukkiyah

LIVING JEWISH VALUES

אַהֲבַת צִיּוֹן

Ahavat Tzion
Love of Israel

We express our commitment to the Land of Israel by fulfilling the mitzvah of Ahavat Tzion, which teaches us to love and remember Israel, the Land of Zion. When we visit Israel, plant trees to help rebuild the land, and celebrate the State of Israel's Independence Day, Yom Ha'atzma'ut, we are observing Ahavat Tzion. We recite words of love for Eretz Yisrael in prayers such as the Amidah and the Birkat Hamazon, Grace After Meals.

How can you observe the mitzvah of Ahavat Tzion?

_____

_____

_____

_____

L.J.V.

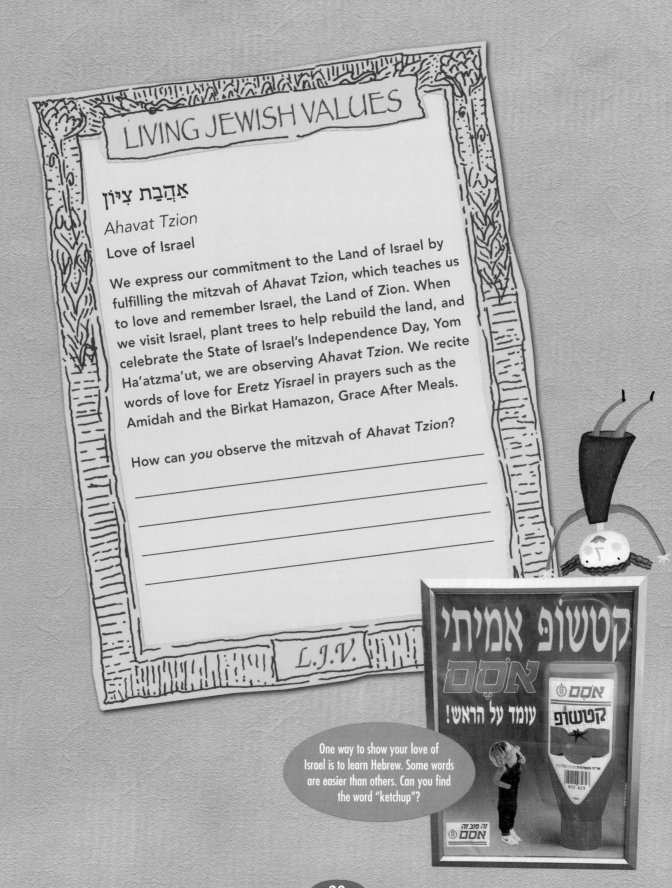

One way to show your love of Israel is to learn Hebrew. Some words are easier than others. Can you find the word "ketchup"?

20

Road Trip!

Let's take a tour of Israel. If we want to go from the north to the south of Israel while spending as little time as possible on the bus, in what order should we visit these cities?

Safed, Jerusalem, Beersheva, Herzliya, Haifa, Caesarea

Look at the map of Israel on page 4.

1. _____
2. _____
3. _____
4. _____
5. _____
6. _____

Israelis do not use dollars to pay for what they buy. They use the New Israeli Shekel (NIS). There are 100 agorot (plural of agorah) to a shekel—just like pennies to a dollar!

The book of Genesis teaches that Abraham bought a plot of land for 400 shekels. Had they been New Israeli Shekels, how many agorot would Abraham have paid?

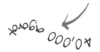

Ugh! I hate math.

Modern Hebrew

For hundreds of years, Jews throughout the world spoke and read Hebrew only when praying or studying holy texts. In their daily lives—when they worked, shopped, studied math, played, or ate—they spoke the languages of the countries in which they lived, or they spoke Jewish forms of those languages, such as Yiddish, a Jewish form of German, or Ladino, a Jewish form of Spanish.

In 1881, Eliezer Ben-Yehuda and his family left Russia and settled in *Eretz Yisrael*. Ben-Yehuda and his wife Deborah believed that Hebrew should be used in everyday life. They published the first Hebrew newspaper in the land. But many people didn't take the idea of speaking conversational Hebrew seriously. How could they be expected to speak an ancient language that didn't have words for such modern inventions as the elevator and the steamship?

So Ben-Yehuda created new words from old ones, and Hebrew once again became a living language. Because of Ben-Yehuda's efforts, Jews around the world now have a common language in which to discuss everything from the Bible to soccer to computers to politics to the latest action movie.

A Living Miracle

Two thousand years ago *Eretz Yisrael* was destroyed; one hundred years ago it was just an idea; today *Medinat Yisrael* is a living miracle! No wonder Jews around the world celebrate Yom Ha'atzma'ut with great joy and sing "Hatikvah" with a full heart.

In almost every Israeli town and city there is a Ben-Yehuda Street, named in honor of the father of modern Hebrew. This Ben-Yehuda Street is in Jerusalem. The street sign is written in Hebrew, Arabic, and English.

Eliezer Ben-Yehuda

Eliezer Ben-Yehuda insisted that his family speak only Hebrew in their home. His son, Itamar, was the first child to grow up speaking modern Hebrew.

23

Borrow and Build

No word for "automobile"? No problem. Ben-Yehuda created the word mechonit by borrowing from the English word "machine."

No word for "newspaper"? Try iton, which Ben-Yehuda based on the Hebrew root meaning "times," as in The New York Times.

In 1966, the Israeli author S.Y. Agnon won the Nobel Prize for literature. It was the first Nobel Prize to be awarded to a Hebrew writer.

I want to win a Nobel Prize, too!

My HEBREW DICTIONARY

שָׁלוֹם	peace, hello, goodbye
מְדִינַת יִשְׂרָאֵל	the State of Israel
אֶרֶץ יִשְׂרָאֵל	the Land of Israel
חֲלוּצִים	pioneers
עִבְרִית	Hebrew
יוֹם הַזִּכָּרוֹן	Memorial Day
יוֹם הָעַצְמָאוּת	Independence Day

Shalom comes from the same root as *shalem*, which means "whole" or "complete." Our tradition teaches that without peace our world cannot be complete.

Shalom,

I just got here, but I've already learned so much about Israel. I can tell this is going to be an interesting trip!

Did you know that Israel is a small country—only about the size of _____ ?

Although it is a modern country, Israel is also very old and is sometimes called_____ .

The Israeli parliament is called the _____ , and the leader of the country is not the president, but the _____ . I also learned that Israel's flag has a _____ in the middle, and that Israel's unit of money is the _____ , not the dollar.

There is a _____ Street in almost every town and city in Israel! Want to know why? Because _____ .

I can't wait to show you my photos. L'hitra'ot! See you soon!

The People
of Israel

This picture of my family was taken at my Aunt Livana and Uncle Amir's wedding. I was born in Israel, which makes me a sabra. Sabra is also the name of the fruit of a cactus. Just like the fruit, we sabras are said to be prickly on the outside but sweet on the inside. In my family, being a sabra makes me special, because most of the family was born somewhere else.

My grandparents came from Poland , but my parents were born in South Africa. My Aunt Monica comes from Holland, while my Uncle Yossi was born in Canada. My cousin Tali is married to Shlomo, who was born in Morocco. Everyone came from different parts of the world, but now we are all Israelis.

me, Liat
Natan
my grandparents
my parents
Uncle Amir
Aunt Livana
Aunt Monica
Uncle Yossi
Tali
Shlomo

A Land of Immigrants

Israel is a land of immigrants. When it was established as a modern state in 1948, only 650,000 Jews were living there. The new country immediately welcomed Jews from outside of Israel who wanted to come and live in the new state. The Law of Return, passed by the Israeli government in 1949, gave every Jew the right to Israeli citizenship. Hundreds of thousands of European Holocaust survivors and refugees from Arab lands flocked to Israel, almost doubling its Jewish population within three years. In 1958, just ten years after its establishment, Israel's Jewish population was more than 2 million.

For decades the Jews of the former Soviet Union suffered from anti-Semitism, poverty, and oppression under the communist goverment. With the help of the Jewish communities of Israel and North America, hundreds of thousands of Russians were able to make *aliyah* in the 1980s and 1990s. These Russian immigrants are studying Hebrew in a class called an *ulpan*.

Today, almost 5 million Jews live in Israel. There are also about 1 million non-Jews, largely Israeli Arabs, living in Israel. More Jews continue to immigrate to Israel from all over the world. This is called making **aliyah,** or "going up."

Cactus with sabras growing on it

In 1949, more than 50,000 Jews from Yemen were flown to Israel as part of Operation Magic Carpet. The Yemenite Jews were so overjoyed to have escaped persecution in their native country that many kissed the ground when they landed. But the new immigrants had much to learn about modern living. Many had lived in such poverty that they had never had indoor plumbing, cars, or telephones.

LIVING JEWISH VALUES

כָּל יִשְׂרָאֵל עֲרֵבִין זֶה בָּזֶה

Kol Yisrael Areivin Zeh Bazeh

All Jews Are Responsible for One Another

Israel's population grew so quickly that the country was unprepared for its new citizens. Many people had to live in tents while they looked for jobs, learned Hebrew, and made friends. Jews around the world provided money, food, and other assistance to help settle these people. Their concern is an example of *Kol Yisrael Areivin Zeh Bazeh*, which is the belief that all Jews are responsible for one another.

Do you know any people or organizations that help care for Jews in need? What are their names, and how do they help?

_____

_____

_____

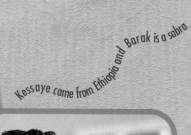

Kessaye came from Ethiopia and Barak is a sabra

Shulah came from Yemen.

Did You Know?

- There are more newspapers in different languages per square mile in Israel than in any other country in the world.

- Movies from all over the world are shown in Israel, with translations called subtitles at the bottom of the screen. The subtitles appear in many languages, including Hebrew, Russian, Arabic, French, and English.

One People, Many Differences

Each immigrant group has come to Israel with its own traditions, foods, languages, music, and stories. Jews from Romania, for example, feast on blintzes, while Jews from Iraq enjoy *nanaeya*, a tasty dish of meatballs with minty sweet-and-sour sauce. Even though we are all Jews, sometimes we have trouble understanding one another. When they arrived in Israel, the Brazilian Jews spoke Portuguese and couldn't understand the Dutch Jews, who in turn couldn't understand a word of the Amharic language spoken by the Ethiopian Jews.

Jews from Western and Eastern Europe are known as Ashkenazim, while Jews from Portugal, Spain, and other Mediterranean countries are called Sephardim. Sephardim who come from Middle Eastern countries such as Yemen, Syria, Morocco, and Iraq are called *Edot Hamizrah*, or Easterners. Although these communities may differ in their complexions, their dress, and their foods, they are united in their common home: Israel.

Nissim came from Argentina.

Emanuel came from the United States.

Michal and Sigal came from France.

An Immigration Story: Ethiopian Jews

For centuries, Jews lived in Ethiopia but were cut off from the rest of our people. When Ethiopia suffered a great famine and war in the 1980s, the Jews became especially eager to leave. In 1984, the Israeli government and Jewish organizations from North America worked together with the Israeli airline, El Al, to fly the hopeful immigrants from Ethiopia to Israel. Because the Ethiopian government did not want the world to know that almost 8,000 of its citizens were fleeing the country, the rescue mission had to be conducted in secret.

The mission to bring the Ethiopian Jews to Israel continued into the 1990s. Almost the entire Jewish community of Ethiopia has been brought to Israel. Today, more than 56,000 Ethiopians live in the Jewish state.

The 1984 airlift of Ethiopian Jews to Israel was called Operation Moses. Why do you think it was given that name?

Africa and the Middle East

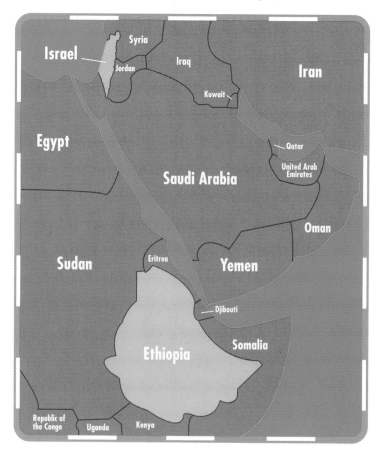

Ethiopia is 2,000 miles from Israel!

What Is a Jewish State?

Jews around the world celebrated the creation of *Medinat Yisrael,* the first Jewish state in almost 2,000 years. But no one knew what a modern Jewish state should be like. Should only Jews be citizens? Should non-Jews have no rights? Should the prime minister be a rabbi?

What holidays should be celebrated in a Jewish state? only Jewish holidays? mostly Jewish holidays? no religious holidays? Should restaurants serve only kosher food? Should bakeries be forced to close on Yom Kippur and to sell only matzah on Passover?

These are just some of the many questions the founders of *Medinat Yisrael* had to think about. Some questions were easier to answer than others. For example, because Israel is a modern democracy, people of all races and religions can become citizens, and their rights are protected by Israeli law. Because Israel is a Jewish state, Jewish holidays are national holidays. For instance, on Rosh Hashanah and Yom Kippur schools and businesses close. And on Purim, adults and children dressed in costumes and masks parade through the streets of Israel.

Israel's Declaration of Independence proclaims that the values of the State of Israel are to be based on the lessons of "liberty, justice, and peace that were taught by the Jewish prophets." Can you name two of our prophets?

_____

_____

The majority of Israeli Jews—about 60 percent—observe at least some religious traditions. For example, they may eat kosher food, attend a seder, and go to synagogue on the High Holidays. Twenty percent of Israeli Jews are nonobservant, or secular; another 20 percent are Orthodox, or strictly observant of traditional Jewish laws and customs. As in other countries, there are differences among Orthodox Jews. Some—the modern Orthodox—are more liberal in their observance, and some—the ultra-Orthodox—are more traditional.

Israelis of all races, religions, and beliefs must learn to live together in peace and harmony.

But some questions are more difficult to answer, and Israelis struggle with them even today. Like Jews in other countries, Israeli Jews do not always agree on how to live as Jews. For example, nonobservant, or secular, Israeli Jews study the Bible and other holy texts to learn the culture, history, legends, and values of the Jewish people. But they do not want the government to tell them what they can and cannot eat, how—or if—they must pray, or how to spend their time on Shabbat, Yom Kippur, or Passover.

Other Jews, among them very observant, or ultra-Orthodox, Jews called Ḥaredim, believe that traditional Jewish law, or **halachah**, should be the law of Israel. For example, the Ḥaredim want the Knesset to pass laws declaring that all stores owned by Israeli Jews must be closed on Shabbat, that all Jewish butchers must sell only kosher meat, and that Jewish men and women should pray separately at Israel's holy places. Although these Jews are a minority, they have a strong influence in the Knesset.

Because Israel does not separate religion and government, sometimes there are clashes between Jews with different beliefs.

El Al, Israel's airline, has transported millions of immigrants and tourists to Israel. Do you think it should be permitted to schedule flights on Shabbat and on other Jewish holy days? Explain your answer.

_____

_____

_____

_____

_____

Do you think that restaurants in Israel should serve only kosher food? Why or why not?

_____

_____

_____

Other Religions

Although Israel is the homeland of the Jewish people, many people of other faiths also live there and consider Israel a holy land. Almost 1 million Arabs live in Israel. Most practice the religion of Islam and are called Muslims. A smaller number of Arabs are Christians.

Members of all religious groups can become Israeli citizens. They can vote and can be elected to the Knesset. Israel's Declaration of Independence ensures freedom of religion for all its citizens. Israeli law protects the holy places of all religions and allows worshippers access to these important sites.

The Druze people also make their home in Israel. The Druze religion broke away from Islam in the eleventh century. While most young Druze dress like other Israelis, some adults distinguish themselves with their striking black-and-white clothes. The Druze speak Arabic, and they support the State of Israel because it offers them religious freedom.

Muslims consider Jerusalem one of the holiest places in the world. It is home to the Al Aksa Mosque, Jerusalem's main place of Islamic worship. Just a few feet away from Al Aksa is another famous mosque, the Dome of the Rock, shown here.

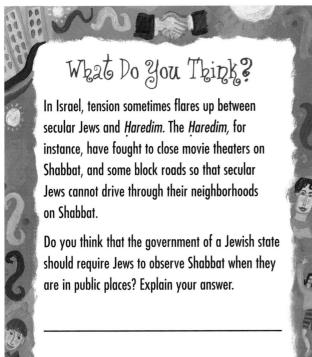

What Do You Think?

In Israel, tension sometimes flares up between secular Jews and Ḥaredim. The Ḥaredim, for instance, have fought to close movie theaters on Shabbat, and some block roads so that secular Jews cannot drive through their neighborhoods on Shabbat.

Do you think that the government of a Jewish state should require Jews to observe Shabbat when they are in public places? Explain your answer.

_____

_____

_____

IT'S A FACT

- When Israel was established in 1948, it offered all the Arabs living there full citizenship, including the right to vote and the right to hold office in the Knesset.

- In 1999, Abdel Raḥman Zuabi became the first Israeli Arab to be appointed to Israel's Supreme Court.

Many Peoples, *One Country*

Israel is the homeland of the Jews and the home of many other people. Immigrants from all over the world and citizens from different backgrounds have had to learn to get along and work together to help Israel become a strong, democratic nation.

study this today!

Miss Israel

In 1999, Rana Raslan was crowned Miss Israel. She was the first Arab woman ever to receive that honor. "It does not matter if I am Jewish or Arab," she said. "I will represent Israel as best as I can." Rana stressed how important it is for Arabs and Jews to live together in peace.

Rana Raslan, Israel's Beauty Queen, *Malkat Hayofi*

My HEBREW DICTIONARY

עֲלִיָּה   going up

הֲלָכָה   Jewish Law

The honor of being called to the Torah is called an *aliyah*. When Jews from the Diaspora move to Israel, we say that they have "made *aliyah*." Why do you think the same word is used to describe these two actions?

it is compared to going up and reading the torah

She's not just beautiful. She's smart!

34

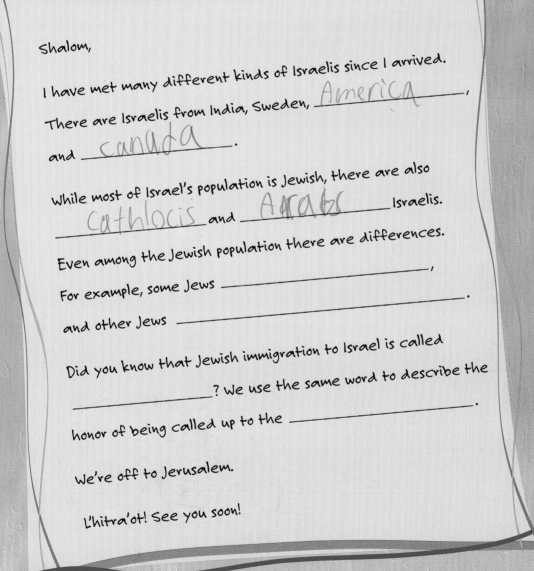

Tell your friend about the different kinds of people who live in Israel.

Shalom,

I have met many different kinds of Israelis since I arrived. There are Israelis from India, Sweden, _America_, and _canada_.

While most of Israel's population is Jewish, there are also _cathlocis_ and _Arabs_ Israelis. Even among the Jewish population there are differences. For example, some Jews _____, and other Jews _____.

Did you know that Jewish immigration to Israel is called _____? We use the same word to describe the honor of being called up to the _____.

We're off to Jerusalem.

L'hitra'ot! See you soon!

3 Jerusalem, City of Gold

Shalom, and welcome to Jerusalem! I'm Ḥagai. Liat and I go to soccer camp together. When I heard that you wanted a tour of Jerusalem, I volunteered to be your guide! My family has lived in Jerusalem for seven generations, and we are proud to be part of the city's history.

Most of the buildings here are built from Jerusalem stone. The stones look almost golden in daylight, but sunset gives them a beautiful pink glow. My grandfather says that each stone in Jerusalem has a story to tell. I think he means that because the stones are very old, they have seen history being made.

My grandfather

This is me, Ḥagai

A *City* Unlike Any Other

There is a city in Israel unlike any other in the world. For centuries, its beauty and glory have inspired poets, musicians, and sages. While the city is thousands of years old, much of it is very new. Traffic jams sometimes occur as cars try to pass someone on a donkey that is trotting slowly along the winding streets. Shopping malls are built on top of ancient hills, and apartment buildings rise over the silent remains of a city that bustled 2,000 years ago.

The city is Jerusalem—**Yerushalayim.**

Over 3,000 years ago, King David made Jerusalem the capital and religious center of ancient Israel. After his death, his son, King Solomon, built the Holy Temple, or **Beit Hamikdash,** on Mount Moriah in Jerusalem to house the Ark of the Covenant. As it says in the Bible, "I [Solomon] have built the House for the name of Adonai, God of Israel. And in it I have put the Ark, in which is the Covenant Adonai made with the children of Israel" (2 Chronicles 6:10–11).

In Jerusalem, sometimes you compete with donkeys for a parking space!

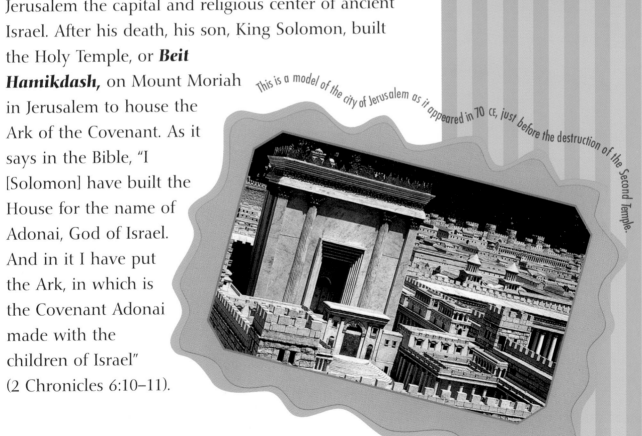

This is a model of the city of Jerusalem as it appeared in 70 CE, just before the destruction of the Second Temple.

The Talmud teaches that God gave ten measures of beauty to the world. Jerusalem took nine, and the rest of the world got just one. What do you think this Talmudic saying means?

LIVING JEWISH VALUES

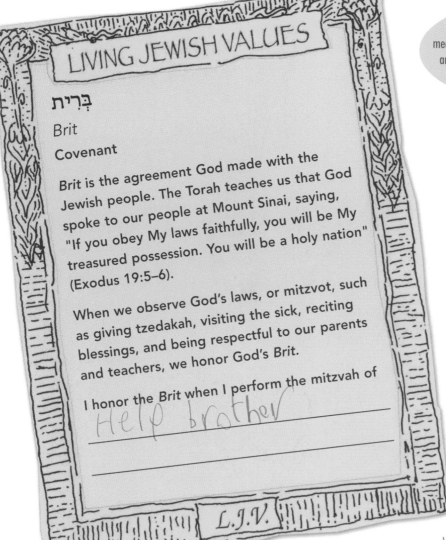

בְּרִית

Brit

Covenant

Brit is the agreement God made with the Jewish people. The Torah teaches us that God spoke to our people at Mount Sinai, saying, "If you obey My laws faithfully, you will be My treasured possession. You will be a holy nation" (Exodus 19:5–6).

When we observe God's laws, or mitzvot, such as giving tzedakah, visiting the sick, reciting blessings, and being respectful to our parents and teachers, we honor God's Brit.

I honor the Brit when I perform the mitzvah of

Help brother

L.J.V.

An orchestra practicing on a quiet Jerusalem hillside

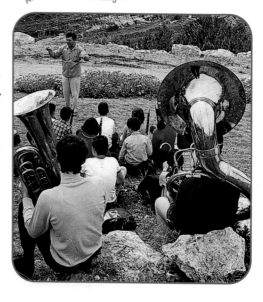

Our tradition teaches that wherever we pray, we face toward Jerusalem because the Temple was there. And we end the Passover seder by saying, "Next year in Jerusalem!"

Jerusalem is built on several mountains. From the west and east, the roads leading to the city are curved and steep. As you drive up, you can feel the car struggling to reach the top. The modern part of the city spreads out for miles and miles, and there are buildings as far as the eye can see.

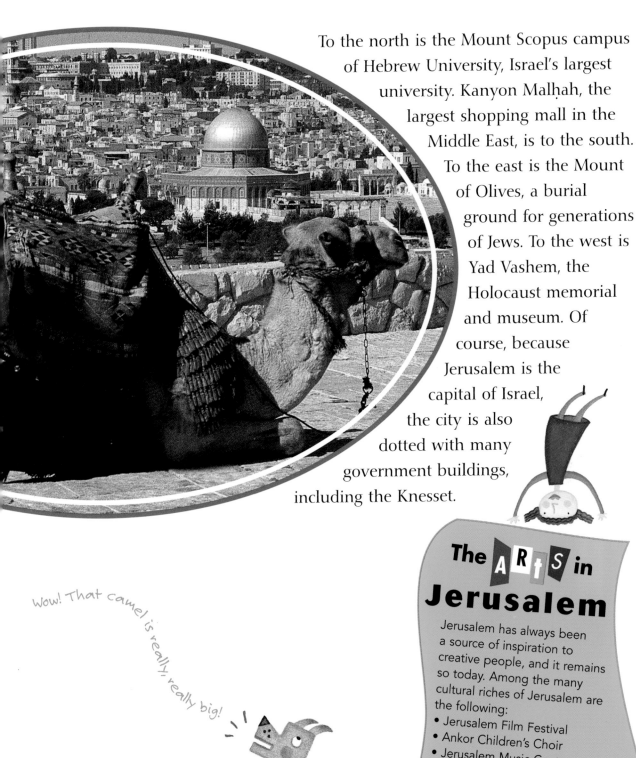

To the north is the Mount Scopus campus of Hebrew University, Israel's largest university. Kanyon Malḥah, the largest shopping mall in the Middle East, is to the south. To the east is the Mount of Olives, a burial ground for generations of Jews. To the west is Yad Vashem, the Holocaust memorial and museum. Of course, because Jerusalem is the capital of Israel, the city is also dotted with many government buildings, including the Knesset.

Wow! That camel is really, really big!

The ARtS in Jerusalem

Jerusalem has always been a source of inspiration to creative people, and it remains so today. Among the many cultural riches of Jerusalem are the following:

- Jerusalem Film Festival
- Ankor Children's Choir
- Jerusalem Music Center
- Israel Museum
- International Book Fair
- Train Puppet Theater
- Jerusalem Theater
- Bezalel Academy of Arts and Design

Like any big city, Jerusalem is made up of many neighborhoods. The Old City and the New City show the two sides of Jerusalem—ancient and modern.

A Divided City

After the War of Independence in 1948, Jerusalem became a divided city. While Israel controlled the western half of the city, Jordan controlled the eastern half, including the Old City. Jews were not permitted to live or visit there.

It was not until the Six-Day War in 1967, when the Israeli army gained control of the eastern part of the city, that Jerusalem was reunited. Walls built in 1948 were torn down; roads were built to connect the two parts of the city. The Jewish people could once again live, visit, and worship in the Old City. Most importantly, we could pray at the Western Wall!

An Israeli soldier praying at the Western Wall

The Old City

The most famous part of Jerusalem is the Old City, a city within walls first built 3,000 years ago. Its narrow and winding streets are lined with shops, homes, schools, synagogues, churches, mosques, and museums. The Old City is divided into four sections: the Jewish Quarter, the Armenian Quarter, the Christian Quarter, and the Muslim Quarter. The winding roads are brimming with vendors offering jewelry, pottery, postcards, and gifts. Carts filled with fresh, warm pita bread and sweet pastries, sticky with honey and almonds, tempt passersby with their delicious aromas.

Let's take a stroll through the streets of Jerusalem!

Tower of David

Next to the Jaffa Gate entrance to the Old City is the Tower of David, which once was a fortress and now houses a museum that is dedicated to the history of Jerusalem.

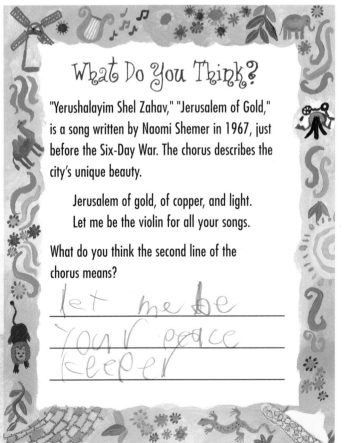

What Do You Think?

"Yerushalayim Shel Zahav," "Jerusalem of Gold," is a song written by Naomi Shemer in 1967, just before the Six-Day War. The chorus describes the city's unique beauty.

> Jerusalem of gold, of copper, and light.
> Let me be the violin for all your songs.

What do you think the second line of the chorus means?

let me be
your peace
keeper

The Old City's open air market, or shuk, is filled with interesting crafts, such as these embroidered dresses.

We can enter the Old City through the Jaffa Gate, one of the busiest of the seven open gates that are built into the Old City's walls. First we pass the Tower of David, then continue down a narrow street and down the hill, until we turn right to reach the Western Wall, or **Hakotel Hama'aravi.** The Western Wall is a supporting wall of the Second Temple. It is often referred to simply as *Hakotel,* or the Wall.

Some people call the Kotel the "Wailing Wall," because many Jews have cried when they prayed there.

Today, many people visit the Kotel to remember all that has happened in Jewish history, to pray for the future of the Jewish people and all Creation, and to feel closer to God.

In *Eretz Yisrael*, you don't just read about our ancestors, you stand where they stood and see what they saw.

The Old City is an archaeologist's dream because there is so much history waiting to be discovered there. For instance, the Ophel Archaeological Garden reveals a massive network of ancient underground tunnels and entire blocks of Jerusalem's main street as they stood 2,000 years ago.

Thanks to the efforts of teams of archaeologists, visitors to the garden can now have an idea of how the city looked at the time of its destruction by the Romans in 70 CE.

Archaeology is the study of the artifacts, or remains, of earlier cultures. These artifacts may include items such as tools, wall paintings, and pottery. Archaeologists, the people who study these remains, help us learn more about history and the lives of the people who came before us.

Montefiore's Windmill

The Shrine of the Book was designed to look like the clay jars in which the Dead Sea Scrolls were found.

The New City

The New City of Jerusalem surrounds the walls of the Old City. It is filled with must-see places to visit. Here are just a few.

Montefiore's Windmill When Sir Moses Montefiore, a wealthy British Jew, visited Jerusalem in the mid-1800s, he was horrified by the crowded, unsanitary conditions in the Old City. Hoping to improve the living conditions of Jerusalem's Jews, in 1860 he established Mishkenot She'ananim, a modern settlement outside of its walls.

Israel Museum The Israel Museum has many interesting exhibitions—from ancient coins and pottery to displays of modern painting and sculpture. Its holdings include work by Israeli artists, such as Shoshana Heimann, Yosse Stern, and Asim Abu-Shakra, and pieces by international masters such as Rembrandt, Pablo Picasso, and Andy Warhol. The museum's collection also includes Jewish ceremonial objects as well as wedding clothes worn by Jewish brides and grooms from around the world.

The Shrine of the Book is a separate building that houses the Dead Sea Scrolls. More than 2,000 years old, the scrolls are the oldest known Jewish religious manuscripts. Near the Shrine of the Book is the open-air Billy Rose Sculpture Garden, which includes the work of many internationally famous artists.

Tisch Gardens Biblical Zoo The Tisch Gardens Biblical Zoo is home to a fascinating collection of creatures, many of which are mentioned in the Bible. These birds, mammals, and reptiles are the living, breathing connections between today and biblical times, and you can visit them in Jerusalem. Don't miss the griffon vultures, white oryxes, and leopards!

The beauty of Jerusalem's Billy Rose Sculpture Garden can make you dance with joy.

Tisch Gardens Biblical Zoo

In 1953, the Israeli government declared that a memorial to the victims of the Holocaust would be built in Jerusalem. This is the entrance to the Children's Memorial at Yad Vashem.

Yad Vashem Jerusalem is also home to Yad Vashem, a memorial, museum, and research library dedicated both to the Jews who were murdered in the Holocaust and to the heroic people who risked their lives to save Jews. The Avenue of the Righteous Gentiles honors the non-Jewish heroes who showed such bravery.

The Children's Memorial of Yad Vashem is dedicated to the memory of the children who died in the Holocaust. It is a theater, dark except for many tiny points of light, or "stars." Each star represents the life of a child who was killed in the Holocaust. The children's names are continuously read aloud on an audiotape so that their memory is kept alive.

Parks An important part of Jerusalem is its many beautiful parks, which offer Israelis and tourists space to relax and enjoy the city. Jerusalemites love to stroll in their parks on Shabbat and holidays, especially in the spring, when the tulips are in bloom.

Gan Hapa'amon, or Liberty Bell Park, honors the 1976 bicentennial—the two hundredth birthday—of the United States. It has a model of Philadelphia's Liberty Bell. A roller-skating rink forms the center of the park, or **gan**, and there are lots of fun structures to climb, including Jerry, the large green dragon.

Gan Havradim, near the Knesset and Supreme Court, is a garden filled with roses from around the world. *Gan Sacher* on Ben Tzvi Boulevard has a fitness track and a skating rink. And *Gan San Simon* is on the spot where one of the most dramatic battles of the Israeli War of Independence took place. The park has a bunker and a real tank, as well as a basketball court. But you can have the most fun in Kiryat Hayovel, for it has the Monster Sculpture. The Monster— it's called *Mifletzet* in Hebrew—has three tongues coming out of its mouth. Each tongue is a slide!

The word *mifletzet* appears in the Bible's book of Kings. In Israel, even when you are at play, your words connect you to Jewish tradition.

You can learn to say it in Hebrew!

Sorry, we have to get back on the bus. I know we haven't had time to go to the Botanical Gardens, the Museum of Natural History, the Cable Car Museum, the Magic Road, the Bible Lands Museum, the Bloomfield Science Museum, the Coin Exhibit, the ICCY Doll Collection, the Nekker Glass Factory, the Givat Mordechai Firehouse, or the Eyn Yael Living Museum, where you can hike, ride donkeys, milk sheep, bake bread, and make pottery. But that's okay, because you can come back to Israel next year, and the year after that, and the year after that. . . .

My HEBREW DICTIONARY

יְרוּשָׁלַיִם	Jerusalem
בֵּית הַמִּקְדָּשׁ	Holy Temple
הַכֹּתֶל הַמַּעֲרָבִי	the Western Wall
גַּן	garden

The ancient sages taught that the name *Yerushalayim* comes from the same Hebrew root as the word *shalom*, which means "peace." Jerusalem is sometimes called "the City of Peace."

There are so many things to see and do, you have to visit Israel more than once!

See what I mean? Liat's so BOSSY. I want to go to the Jerusalem swimming pool! It has a great water slide. And Betar Jerusalem—one of Israel's top soccer teams—is playing Hapoel Jerusalem tonight at the Teddy Stadium. I ABSOLUTELY, POSITIVELY, CANNOT MISS THE GAME.

Hey! Wait for me. I want to go on the Monster again.

If you could choose someone from the Bible to take on a tour of modern Jerusalem, who would you pick? Why? What would you ask them about ancient Israel?

_____

_____

_____

_____

_____

_____

_____

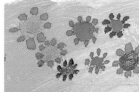

Draw here. You can draw lots of things... →

Greetings from the City of Gold

Send a postcard to a friend. On the front of the card, draw a picture of yourself visiting the sight in Jerusalem that is most interesting to you.

On the back of the card, tell your friend about the many ancient places in Jerusalem and about its modern sites.

AIR MAIL

← Write stuff here.

Salaam! My name is Amal, which is Arabic for "hope." I am an Arab Muslim. This is my friend Uri. He lives in Tel Aviv. When his cousin Liat told us that she was taking you on a tour of Israel, we volunteered to show you the cities by the sea.

Tel Aviv and Haifa are Israel's largest coastal cities. They are both beautiful. But, as nice as Tel Aviv is, I'm glad I live in Haifa. Part of Haifa is built on a mountain, Mount Carmel. To get to my house you have to drive or take the train to the very top of the mountain. From my balcony, I can watch the big ships in Haifa's port. When Uri visits, we like to imagine what each ship is carrying and where it is sailing to.

Pack your bathing suit and join us on a tour of Israel's waterfront cities!

I'm Amal

This is Uri

Greetings from Haifa

Tel Aviv-Jaffa

Located on the Mediterranean Sea, Tel Aviv-Jaffa is busy, noisy, and packed with people, cars, and buses. There are important differences between the ancient section of the city called Jaffa, pronounced *Yafo* in Hebrew, and the section called **Tel Aviv**, which is thoroughly modern.

Jaffa's port is thousands of years old. In fact, ships carrying the cedar trees from Lebanon that were used to build the Temple in Jerusalem were unloaded in Jaffa. By 1909, Jaffa had become so overcrowded that a group of 60 Jewish families set up tents on the sand dunes to the north. This community mushroomed into Tel Aviv, which eventually became Israel's business, cultural, and sports center. In 1949 Jaffa was made part of Tel Aviv, and the city's official name became Tel Aviv-Jaffa.

Bird's Eye View

The best view you can get of Tel Aviv-Jaffa and the Mediterranean coast can be seen from the top-floor observation deck of the Shalom Towers—433 feet high!

Although most of the tower is office space, Israel's first skyscraper is also home to the Israel Wax Museum.

The Bible describes how the ancient Jews returned to Israel from Babylonia—which is now Iraq—and rebuilt the Temple. "They also gave money to the stone cutters and to the carpenters, and food, and drink, and oil, to those of Zidon and Zor to bring cedar trees from Lebanon by sea to Jaffa" (Ezra 3:7).

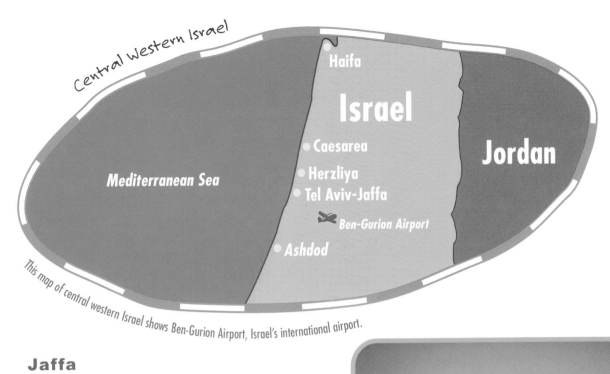

Haifa

Israel

Mediterranean Sea

Caesarea

Herzliya

Tel Aviv-Jaffa

Ben-Gurion Airport

Jordan

Ashdod

This map of central western Israel shows Ben-Gurion Airport, Israel's international airport.

Jaffa

Jaffa's twisty, cobblestone streets wind around each other like a giant maze. The streets are so narrow and crowded that it is easier to walk in this ancient city than to drive. Many of the buildings look as if they have been around for hundreds of years. In fact, archaeologists have discovered objects in Jaffa that are 4,000 years old, making it one of the world's oldest port cities.

The port of Jaffa

The Artists' Quarter is home to many art galleries and studios. As you wander up and down Jaffa's narrow alleys and peek into open doorways, you can see artists at work on paintings and sculpture. The Hebrew word for "beautiful" is *yafeh*—very similar to the name of this ancient and very beautiful seaside community.

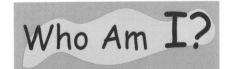

Who Am I?

I am a prophet who set sail from Jaffa. During my trip, I wound up in the belly of a big fish. Do you know my name?

Jonah, "Jonah...went down to Jaffa and he found a ship going to Tarshish..." (Jonah 1:3).

53

In addition to painters and sculptors, gifted craftspeople also live in Jaffa. Many of these silversmiths, ceramic artists, weavers, and glass blowers specialize in beautiful and one-of-a-kind Jewish ritual objects, such as Kiddush cups, ḥallah covers, and Ḥanukkah menorahs.

A picture taken at a Sephardic wedding ceremony in Jaffa in the late 1800s.

Kikar Hasha'on, or Clock Tower Square, is an important Jaffa landmark. When you pass the clock, you know you have left Tel Aviv and entered Jaffa.

Strange but True!

The streets in Jaffa's Artists' Quarter are named after the signs of the zodiac. Ask for directions to a gallery and you might be told to make a left on Leo, turn right on Sagittarius, and then follow Pisces all the way down the hill!

The Modern City of Tel Aviv

Israelis call Tel Aviv the city that never sleeps. One-third of Israel's population lives there and in the surrounding areas. Almost every other Israeli comes to Tel Aviv at least once in a while to enjoy its rich cultural life, do business, swim on its beaches, and take advantage of its many sports facilities.

Tel Aviv is the home of Israel's national theater, Habimah. Habimah was founded in Moscow in 1917; it moved to Tel Aviv in 1928, and the theater was built in 1935. Habimah was the first professional theater company to produce plays in Hebrew. Although it presents plays from around the world, every production is performed in Hebrew. The Israel Philharmonic Orchestra is housed next door to Habimah.

Ḥayyim Naḥman Bialik

Ḥayyim Naḥman Bialik (1873–1934) left Russia to settle in Tel Aviv in 1924. He greatly influenced the development of modern Hebrew and is considered the national poet of Israel. Many of his children's and adult poems have been set to music.

Bialik lived near the Habimah National Theater on what is now called *Reḥov Bialik*, or Bialik Street.

Ḥayyim Naḥman Bialik

There were musicians in biblical times, too. King David played a harp and Miriam—Moses's sister—played a timbrel, a tambourine-like instrument.

Can you imagine seeing Shakespeare's Romeo and Juliet in Hebrew?

Tel Aviv is the home of the Tel Aviv Museum, which has an outstanding collection of Israeli and international art. *Beth Hatefutsoth*, or the Diaspora Museum, is also located in Tel Aviv, on the campus of Tel Aviv University. The museum's exhibits tell the story of 2,500 years of Jewish life in the Diaspora—in Poland, Mexico, the United States, Ethiopia, Japan, Australia, and many more places where Jews have lived and continue to live. Visitors can enjoy the exhibits, research their family trees at the computer center, and view the museum's replica collection of miniature synagogues from around the world.

Can you find the Hebrew word for museum? The name of the city in Hebrew?

THE TEL AVIV MUSEUM מוזיאון תל אביב

Believe It or Not

Fifty percent of the polished diamonds in the world have been polished in Israel.

Map It Out

Israel's independence was declared on May 14, 1948, in what is now Independence Hall in Tel Aviv. Turn to the map on page 4 and label Tel Aviv next to Israel's Declaration of Independence.

Turn to the map on page 4

I always find a lot of cool things at the shuk.

The Shuk

Every city in Israel has at least one *shuk*, or outdoor market. But each *shuk* has its own character. *Shuk Hacarmel* is Tel Aviv's largest market. Its stalls are bursting with fresh fruits, vegetables, cheeses, olives, spices, flowers, and baked goods. Peddlers sell old and new clothing, shoelaces, flashlights, and leather goods.

Jaffa's most popular *shuk* is *Shuk Hapishpeshim*, Hebrew for "flea market." There you can find clothing, jewelry, old coins, rugs, pottery, copper jugs, and used books in a dozen languages.

The Tel Aviv Stock Exchange, founded in 1953, makes Tel Aviv the financial capital of Israel. The Diamond Exchange, where diamonds are bought and sold, is in Ramat Gan, right outside of Tel Aviv.

Today there are malls all over Israel. But for a long time, there was only Dizengoff Center, a large indoor mall in the center of Tel Aviv.

Dizengoff Center is located—where else?—on Dizengoff Street, the main avenue of downtown Tel Aviv. The street is named for the city's first mayor, Meir Dizengoff.

National Footwear?

If there were an official shoe of Israel, it would be the sandal. Because the weather in most of the country is warm much of the year—sometimes well over 90°F—wearing sandals is one way to keep cool. The classic Israeli sandal is made of brown leather with two simple straps, but you can find almost any kind of sandal imaginable in Israel!

Be a Trendsetter

The shops along Dizengoff Street sell many different kinds of sandals. In the space on the right, design a pair that would look great and keep your feet cool in the heat of an Israeli summer.

Dizengoff Center

Dizengoff Center is filled with many stores, restaurants, video arcades, and movie theaters that are similar to the ones in your hometown. For example, while kids from Long Island and Brooklyn are lining up to see the latest Steven Spielberg movie at New York City's Ziegfeld Theater, Israelis are watching it at the Hod Dizengoff Theater!

This sparkling, multicolored fountain marks the center of Dizengoff Circle. The fountain and the colorful moving statue in the middle were designed by the internationally known Israeli artist Yaacov Agam.

Draw here—express yourself.

But, for all that is similar to your hometown, when you are in Dizengoff Center there are things that will remind you that you are in Israel. For example, the doorways to shops and theaters have mezuzot. Store signs and clothing labels are in Hebrew. And the books and magazines in the bookstores—dictionaries, first-aid manuals, cookbooks, and even comic books—open from the "back," because they're in Hebrew too!

The Wonderful World of Tel Aviv Sports!

Among the many sports facilities in Tel Aviv are the following:

- Israel Skating Center
- Israel Tennis Center
- Miniature Golf and Play
- Heichal Hakeraḥ Ice Skating
- Yad Eliyahu Basketball Stadium
- Kiryat Ono Swimming Pool
- Dolphinarium Diving Club
- Park Hadarom Water-Skiing
- Maymadion Water Park
- Ilan Sports Center for the Physically Handicapped

Sasha and Beni, who immigrated to Israel from Russia, are learning how to play tennis at the Israel Tennis Center.

המרכז לטניס בישראל ‏TENNIS CENTER

Finally, I get to swim!

Caesarea

King Herod, who was appointed by the Roman emperor Augustus Caesar to rule Israel, was ancient Israel's greatest builder. In 22 BCE, he completed the majestic port city of Caesarea. The city featured an open-air theater, palaces, temples, a hippodrome, and an aqueduct. More than 100,000 people lived in Herod's Caesarea. It was one of the largest cities in the world at that time.

Herod named Caesarea in honor of the Roman emperor. He spared no expense—never before had such a large artificial harbor been built. The port lasted for over 1,000 years. It became run-down and was restored by the Crusaders—Christian soldiers who conquered the Land of Israel from the Muslims who controlled it 900 years ago.

Caesarea's aqueduct

Did You Know?

- Today, the open-air theater at Caesarea seats 5,000 people and is the site of dance and music performances, including rock concerts and operas.

- Hippodromes are stadiums in which horse and chariot races were held in ancient times. The hippodrome at Caesarea could seat 20,000 people.

- An aqueduct is an artificial channel used to move water.

Check It Out

Want to see Caesarea's original port? You'll have to bring your scuba-diving equipment! The ancient harbor is now completely underwater. Excavations in 1978 showed that Herod's engineers used concrete that could harden in water.

What Do You Think?

Visitors to Caesarea sometimes find old coins or pieces of ancient pottery during their stay. Archaeologists ask them to leave such items behind because they provide important clues to understanding the past. Some visitors ignore these requests and take their finds home.

Why do you think they do this? What might you say to change their minds?

_____

_____

_____

_____

The Crusaders fortified the port with a great moat and huge city walls. While some of the Crusaders' structures, including an unfinished cathedral, have been uncovered by archaeologists, much of ancient Caesarea is still buried under the sand.

Crusader fortress

Today, Caesarea's open-air theater is once again a popular gathering place. In the summertime, concertgoers listen to music, watch the sun set over the Mediterranean, and enjoy the cool sea breeze.

Haifa

On a clear day you can see Haifa from Caesarea. The city sits atop tree-covered Mount Carmel, which slopes down to the blue Mediterranean. Haifa is often compared with San Francisco. Because of their high elevations, both cities offer breathtaking views of the waters below. And driving around these two cities can give you a roller-coaster feeling in the pit of your stomach as the roads make steep downhill drops before suddenly curving back up.

The name of Haifa was first mentioned in the Talmud—the holy texts that contain Jewish law—as a fishing village. Later it was known as a ship-building port. Today, Haifa is Israel's third-largest city, and its harbor at the foot of the mountain is a busy international port. In addition to the import and export businesses that dot the port area, Haifa is also one of Israel's high-tech centers. IBM and Intel are among the many companies that have offices there.

Did You Know?

Obviously, you can't hire a van to move to Israel! Instead, furniture is sent by boat in large containers. Most of the containers are unloaded at the port of Haifa; others are unloaded in Ashdod. Do you remember what moving to Israel is called?

Making aliyah

Ashdod, which is on the coast of Israel, south of Tel Aviv, is Israel's busiest port.

Israel's exports include cut and polished diamonds, computer software, military equipment, electronic components, medical equipment, citrus fruits, flowers, candy, and clothing. High-tech products are Israel's leading export.

In 1902, in his book Old New Land, Theodor Herzl described Haifa as "the city of the future."

Haifa is home to the Technion, also known as the Israel Institute of Technology. The Technion's students specialize in learning about high-tech industries such as computer science, aerospace engineering, and medicine. It is one of five universities in the world where students design, build, and launch their own satellites.

Do you know which city is the largest in Israel and which is the second largest?

Jerusalem is the largest city and Tel Aviv is the second largest.

The Technion's original building is now the site of the Technoda, the National Museum of Science and Technology. Visitors can participate in the interactive exhibits. Last time I went, I learned how e-mail gets to the right electronic address and how cell phones work!

One important area of research in which the Technion has been a leader is water desalination—making salt water fit for agricultural, industrial, and human use.

Haifa is the international center for Baha'i, one of the world's newest religions. There are about 6 million followers of Baha'i in 170 countries. Baha'i was founded in Iran in 1863. Its followers believe in one God and in the unity of all people, and worship nature's beauty. The founder of Baha'i, Husayn Ali, lived near Haifa in Acre, pronounced **Akko** in Hebrew. Although few Baha'i live in Israel, they are required to visit the Baha'i shrine in Haifa at least once in their lifetime.

The golden dome of the Baha'i shrine is one of the most beautiful sights in Haifa.

My HEBREW DICTIONARY

תֵּל אָבִיב   Tel Aviv

עַכּוֹ   Acre

Tel means "hill" or "mound," and *aviv* means "spring." The Hebrew names of the other seasons are: *ḥoref* (winter), *kayitz* (summer), and *stav* (autumn).

Name these seasons in Hebrew: the season in which you were born, your favorite season, and the season in which Ḥanukkah falls.

_____

_____

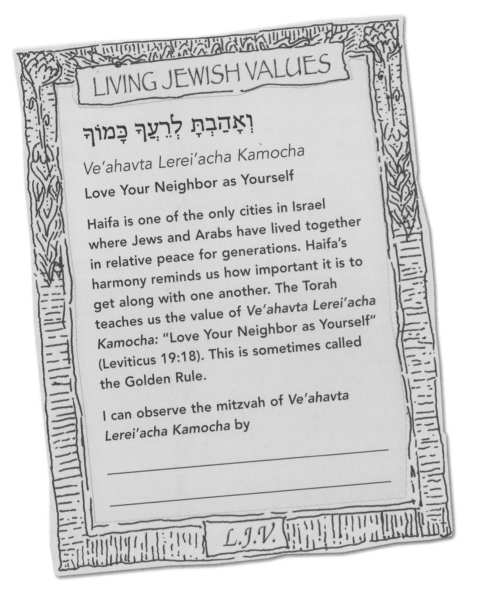

LIVING JEWISH VALUES

וְאָהַבְתָּ לְרֵעֲךָ כָּמוֹךָ

Ve'ahavta Lerei'acha Kamocha

Love Your Neighbor as Yourself

Haifa is one of the only cities in Israel where Jews and Arabs have lived together in relative peace for generations. Haifa's harmony reminds us how important it is to get along with one another. The Torah teaches us the value of Ve'ahavta Lerei'acha Kamocha: "Love Your Neighbor as Yourself" (Leviticus 19:18). This is sometimes called the Golden Rule.

I can observe the mitzvah of Ve'ahavta Lerei'acha Kamocha by

_____

_____

L.J.V.

So Much to See by the Sea

In the days before air travel, visitors to Israel would arrive by boat, docking in one of the coastal cities. Today, Israel's cities on the sea are still busy places. The Tel Aviv-Jaffa area is the heart of Israeli culture and business. Caesarea is the site of one of the most extensive archaeological excavations in the Middle East. And Haifa is a center of technology, industry, and shipping. Of course, Israel's seaside cities also offer great beaches and plenty of fun and excitement!

Although I like living in a modern city, I also like spending time with my grandmother, because she keeps many of the old customs. She is one of the last people in our area to make the thick quilts that keep us warm during cold winter nights. Also, while most people buy lebane, a traditional soft cheese, my grandmother still makes it by hand. She taught me to welcome guests by offering them tea with nana, or mint, and something sweet to eat.

Shalom,

You should "sea" what a great time I'm having in Israel. My friends, Amal and Uri, showed me all around Israel's coastal cities. Our first stop was a two-for-one: _____. _____ is the ancient part of the city. _____ is the modern section, Israel's cultural, business, and sports center.

The Israel Institute of Technology, which is also called the_____, is located in _____, Israel's third largest city and an international port.

The ancient port city of _____ was first built more than 2,000 years ago by _____. Today, _____ work there to uncover clues to the city's ancient history.

When you come, don't forget to pack a bathing suit. All these cities have great _____.

L'hitra'ot! See you soon!

Tell your friends at home about Israel's cities by the sea.

My name is Dalia, and this is my big brother, Ilan. My parents and Ilan came from Ethiopia, but I was born here in Beersheva, right in the middle of the Negev Desert. I like living in the desert because while the days are often warm, the nights are usually cool and comfortable.

I met Liat at an overnight at my friend Devorah's house. Liat and Devorah are cousins. Now the three of us are good friends. So I was happy to help Liat out when she needed a guide for your tour of southern Israel.

Come, let's get started!

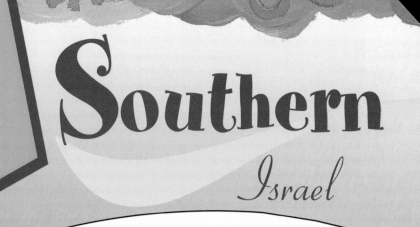

Ilan

Dalia

largest stretch
...up half of the
...10 percent of
...there. *Negev*
...in Hebrew and is also
related to the word "dry." Although the
Negev is a desert, it is not completely
dry—sometimes, streams of water run
through the Negev in winter. The Arava,
the easternmost strip of the Negev, on
the border with Jordan, is a plain
that was created by a split in the
earth's crust millions of years ago.
The northern part of the Arava
runs into the Dead Sea.

Ein Gedi • Dead Sea

Gaza Strip

Masada •

Beersheva •

Sodom •

Israel

Arava Valley

Sinai Desert

Negev

Egypt

Jordan

• Eilat

Which city is near the southern end of the Dead Sea?

Ein Gedi is 12 miles
north of Masada. The Bible tells
us that King David found refuge in
the Ein Gedi desert among "the rocks
of the ibexes." Today, you can still see
herds of ibexes roaming there.
Can you find Ein Gedi on the
map of southern Israel?

The sun is very strong
here, so smear on plenty of
sunscreen, wear sunglasses
and a hat, and drink lots
of water!

The Dead Sea

The Dead Sea is the lowest spot in the world—1,300 feet below sea level. The blue-green water shimmering in the bright sunlight looks inviting—especially on a hot day, when the temperature can reach 120°F. The bad news is that its saltiness makes the water undrinkable and stings your eyes. In fact, the Hebrew name for the Dead Sea is **Yam Hamelaḥ**, the Sea of Salt. The good news is that it is very easy to float in the Dead Sea. In fact, it's impossible to sink!

People from all over Israel and the world flock to the Dead Sea to enjoy its mineral-rich black mud and the hot springs nearby. The waters of the Dead Sea are said to heal rashes, aches, and pains.

Yam Hamelah is called the "Dead Sea" because the water's high salt content makes it impossible for plants or animals to live there.

Even an Olympic swimmer like me can't swim in the Dead Sea!

Salt formations rise out of the Dead Sea and the surrounding land like a sculpture garden. Besides salt, the water is also full of minerals such as potash, magnesium, and bromine. Sulfur fills the air around the Dead Sea with an odor that smells like rotten eggs. Several companies have sprung up in the region to take advantage of the Dead Sea's mineral resources. They produce cosmetics and skin care products, including soaps, lotions, and even facial mud, as well as fertilizer and industrial chemicals. Other companies export the raw minerals to countries across the globe.

Who Am I?

My story is told in Genesis and takes place near Sodom, which is near the Dead Sea, where the tall salt formations look almost like people.

I was warned that if I looked back, I would turn into a pillar of salt. Sure enough, I looked back and became a pillar of salt. Who am I?

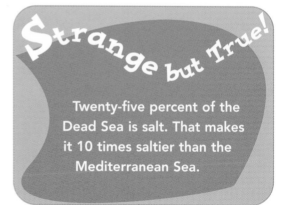

Many salt formations look very beautiful and decorative.

Lot's wife, "But his wife looked back ...and she became a pillar of salt" (Genesis 19:26).

In the Dead Sea, you can just lie back, float, and enjoy a good book!

Masada

Towering 1,000 feet above the Dead Sea is the ancient fortress of Masada. Built on a natural rock formation, Masada stands alone—isolated from other large hills and mountains. For this reason, it made an ideal fortress in earlier times. King Herod built a palace fortress on Masada more than 2,000 years ago.

In 66 CE, as the Romans took control of the land, a group of Jews from Jerusalem escaped to Masada. They held out for several years, until the Romans finally broke down their defenses. Rather than be taken captive, the Jews killed themselves.

Most people take a three-minute cable car ride to the top of Masada. I'd rather make the steep climb up the Snake Path.

King Herod, Master Builder

Appointed by the Roman emperor Augustus Caesar, King Herod governed Israel from 37 BCE until his death in 5 BCE. During his reign, Herod went on a building spree. Many of his projects, including Masada, were reinforced palaces or fortresses designed to protect him from the people he ruled, for he treated them cruelly in his quest for power. Herod named one such fortress Herodion. He also renovated and enlarged the Second Temple in Jerusalem.

Do you remember the name of the coastal city built by Herod?

Caesarea

Here's a hint, the city was named after the emperor who appointed Herod ruler of Israel.

Ask me. I know the answer!

Archaeologists have uncovered the remains of a complete Jewish village on Masada. Their findings include a luxurious palace, a synagogue, a ritual bath, and food and water-storage systems.

71

Beersheva

Beersheva is more than 4,000 years old and is mentioned many times in the Bible. When Israel won its independence in 1948, Beersheva was a hot, sleepy frontier town. It was the last place for miles around to get water, food, and other supplies. There were few buildings and even fewer modern conveniences. The citizens of Beersheva looked as if they had stepped out of a movie about the Wild West: rugged, sunburned, and tough.

The Torah tells us that Jacob "set out with all that was his, and he came to Beersheva, where he offered sacrifices to the God of his father Isaac" (Genesis 46:1). Today, Beersheva is home to Jews from all around the world and to many Bedouin—the nomadic, or wandering, Arab tribes of the desert. This Bedouin woman is wearing a traditional face covering.

There are many fun and interesting places in and around Beersheva, such as the caves of Ḥorvat Za'ak, the Negev Museum, the Ethiopian Arts Center, the Beersheva Arts Center, the Beersheva Theater, the zoo, Luna Negev Amusement Park and Pool, the Tennis Center, the Israel Air Force Museum, Tel Sheva Archaeological Excavations, Kashvan Horseback Riding Center, and Golda Park, where you can fish. But Liat said that there's no time to take you there. You'll have to wait until your next visit to Israel!

IT'S A FACT

- There is an ice-skating rink in Beersheva—a desert city!

- At the Bedouin Heritage Center near Beersheva you can stop for tea, lunch, or dinner and eat a typical Bedouin meal while sitting in a Bedouin tent.

- The animal hospital outside of Beersheva has a camel clinic.

Beersheva has come a long way. Today, Beersheva is one of the largest cities in Israel and the largest in the Negev. Its growth has been helped along by the arrival of thousands of new immigrants from Ethiopia and the former Soviet Union. Beersheva's frontier image has given way to that of a city with modern conveniences and institutions. For example, the Soroka Hospital provides the finest modern medical care.

David Ben-Gurion, Pioneer of the Negev

David Ben-Gurion was a leader in the War of Independence. On May 14, 1948, he proclaimed the founding of the modern State of Israel and became Israel's first prime minister. Ben-Gurion knew that Israel needed to make the best use of all its land—including the desert. He also thought that it was possible to turn the Negev into blooming fields of green. After retiring from politics, Ben-Gurion and his wife, Paula, joined Kibbutz Sde Boker about 20 miles from Beersheva, becoming living examples of how to pioneer the desert.

In his diary, Ben-Gurion copied inspiring words from the Bible: "I will even make a way in the wilderness, and rivers in the desert...to give drink to my people" (Isaiah 43:19–20).

Ben-Gurion University, also called the University of the Negev, is located in Beersheva. Among its many facilities, it has a medical school, animal research center, and computer science program. At the school's desert research center, students continue Ben-Gurion's important work by studying the area's ecology and plant and animal life.

David Ben-Gurion (1886–1973) served as prime minister of Israel for 13 years.

My HEBREW DICTIONARY

נֶגֶב   Negev, south

יָם הַמֶּלַח   Dead Sea, Sea of Salt

בְּאֵר שֶׁבַע   Beersheva

Beersheva means "well of seven" and "well of oath." The Torah teaches us that our patriarch Abraham made an oath with King Abimelech to acquire a well in the Negev. "And so, the place was called Beersheva, for there the two of them swore an oath" (Genesis 21:31).

Eilat

Eilat is located on the southernmost point of Israel, at the northern tip of the Gulf of Eilat. For centuries, it was a caravan stop for travelers and traders crossing continents on their way to Asia, Africa, and Europe. Today, Eilat is a busy port for trade ships arriving from and sailing to Asia and Africa, as well as a year-round vacation resort.

Put on your snorkeling or scuba-diving gear to get a close-up look at the Red Sea's underwater life.

Eilat's underwater observatory has a staircase that takes you 15 feet below sea level to see the magical world of coral reefs, underwater plants, and colorful tropical fish.

Visitors come to Eilat for fun in the sun—snorkeling, sailing, scuba diving, and swimming with dolphins and other sea creatures. Eilat is also a great spot for bird watching, because it is on the main migratory routes from Africa to Asia and Europe. Eagles, storks, buzzards, cranes, and many other varieties of birds can be seen soaring the blue skies of Eilat.

When you're ready for some real excitement, it's time to go parasailing!

Try this riddle: Do you know why birds fly to Africa in the winter?

Because it's too far to walk!

What about this riddle? Do you know how to get down from an Israeli camel?

You don't get down from a camel. You get down from a duck!

75

Map It Out

Visitors to Eilat delight in its warm weather, water sports, underwater scenery, and beautiful beaches. Eilat also has an ostrich farm, a marine nature reserve, and a resort where you can swim with the dolphins! Turn to the map on page 4 and label Eilat by writing its name next to the dolphin.

What countries are close to Eilat?

_____

_____

How about this one: How much fun can you have in southern Israel?

Eilat.

Did You Know?

King Solomon built a port near Eilat. You can read about it in the Bible: "King Solomon built a fleet of ships in Etzion-Gever, which is next to Eilat, on the shore of the Red Sea" (I Kings 9:26). Legend teaches that Solomon first met the Queen of Sheba there.

Look at this.

Want to make a few new friends? No problem—you're always welcome to swim with the dolphins!

The Arava

The road from Eilat to Jerusalem passes through a desert plain called the Arava. The Arava River marks the border between Jordan and Israel, and is bound by two mountain ranges, one in each country. At sunrise, to the east, Jordan's Edom Mountains blaze in the reflection of the sun. At sunset, to the west, Israel's Eilat Mountains take on a fiery glow. Spread throughout the valley are small kibbutzim and moshavim—collective farms. The kibbutz and moshav members work hard planting fields, often in intense heat, helping to give life to Ben-Gurion's dream of a blooming desert. Tourism and industry also provide important sources of income, and Kibbutz Yotvata is known throughout Israel for its large dairy.

What Do You Think?

So far, which place in southern Israel is your favorite? Explain why.

_____

_____

_____

_____

_____

_____

The Arava may be hot and dusty, but at least you won't get caught in a traffic jam.

How about biking in the Arava?

LIVING JEWISH VALUES

בַּל תַּשְׁחִית

Bal Tashḥit

Do Not Destroy

Bal Tashḥit means "do not destroy." This mitzvah teaches that it is people's responsibility to care for nature's resources by not being wasteful or destructive. We can fulfill the mitzvah of Bal Tashḥit in many ways. Irrigating and planting fields is one way to care for the environment. Other ways include turning off lights when we leave a room; recycling glass, aluminum, plastic, and paper rather than throwing out these items; and watering house-plants so they can grow.

List two more ways to observe the mitzvah of Bal Tashḥit.

_____

_____

_____

Read this. ➜

The Hai Bar Nature Reserve is home to animals that have lived in the Negev since biblical times. These are striped-legged wild donkeys.

Desert Sites

The Negev is full of fascinating places to visit. For example, there are three spectacular craters that were formed millions of years ago from huge cracks in the earth's surface. Each crater, or *machtesh*, is a deep valley with steep cliffs on all sides and one water drain. Cut deep into the earth's crust, the sides of the craters look like rainbow-striped sand sculptures.

Not far from Eilat is Timna Valley Park, the site of copper mines that date back to long before King Solomon. The awesome cliffs, canyons, and rock formations were sculpted by nature—the result of many thousands of years of water, wind, and extreme changes in temperature.

The Wonders of Southern Israel

The natural world of southern Israel is unique and beautiful. Whether diving with the dolphins, rock climbing on ancient cliffs, or going on a Jeep safari or a camel caravan, a trip to the south is sure to offer new experiences—once-in-a-lifetime memories that could happen only in Israel.

Machtesh Ramon, the largest of the Negev's craters, is 6 miles across and 25 miles long.

The natural arches at Timna Valley Park are made of red sandstone.

Next time I'm bringing my rock-climbing gear.

79

Shalom,

Southern Israel is amazing! Most of it is covered by the
_____ Desert, which takes up half the land
of Israel.

I tried to swim in the _____, but the water is so
_____ that I could only float! Next, we drove
through a desert plain called the _____
on our way to _____, on Israel's southern tip.
I had a great time. I enjoyed visiting _____
because _____
_____.

We also stopped in _____, which is known as
the capital of the Negev, to tour _____
University. The most interesting fact I learned about
southern Israel is _____
_____.

I can't wait to show you pictures of the beautiful desert.

L'hitra'ot! See you soon!

Shalom! My name is Tamar. I live on Deganyah Alef, a kibbutz in northern Israel. What is a kibbutz? It is a village where people share property and live and work together. Although only 2 percent of Israelis live on kibbutzim—that's plural for kibbutz—they have played an important part in building our country. But I'll tell you more about kibbutz later.

Northern Israel is dotted with Jewish, Arab, and Druze villages. Many people here are farmers. At my kibbutz we have orchards, a dairy, a hen house, and an industrial diamond factory.

I met Liat last year when she visited her relatives here. She's been back several times, and we've become good friends. I'm happy she told me about you so that I can show you around northern Israel.

Liat

Tamar

HEN HOUSE

Water Is Precious

Israelis have a special respect for water—***mayim***. Why? Because half the country is desert, maintaining an adequate water supply has always been difficult. The Hermon and the Upper Galilee, with its high mountains, green valleys, and running rivers, provide one-third of Israel's water. Water from snow and rain flow down Mount Hermon, feeding the Jordan River and its tributaries. Through a network of pumping stations, reservoirs, canals, and pipelines, water from the north is carried to the rest of the country.

This waterfall is at the source of the Jordan River.

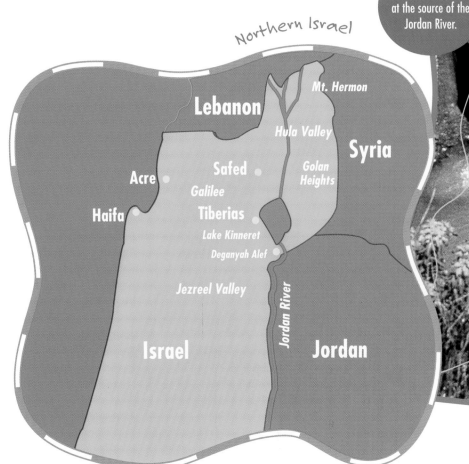

Northern Israel

Locate the Jordan River on this map.

The Hula and Jezreel Valleys

The Hula Valley was once a swampland centered around a lake. *Ḥalutzim* arrived in the Galilee—or **Hagalil** in Hebrew—in the late 1800s. These early pioneers settled in the villages that had been established by Baron Edmond de Rothschild, a wealthy and generous Jew from France. The lives of the pioneers were difficult. Many died of malaria carried by the mosquitoes swarming in the marshes. By 1951, the lake and the surrounding swamp were largely drained. A number of farms, fish ponds, and villages have since been established in the Hula Valley.

The Jezreel Valley—which often is called, simply, *Ha'emek*, or the Valley—is the largest valley in Israel and one of the country's most fertile areas. Like the Hula Valley, the Jezreel Valley had many malarial swamps, but today it is a lush farm region. The commercial center of the Jezreel Valley is the city of Afula.

You can tour the Galilee by hiking, cycling, or riding horseback, or by Jeep. For a wet and wild adventure, take a kayak or raft down the Jordan River.

Jews around the world donate money to the Jewish National Fund to plant trees in Israel, in memory of loved ones who have died and in honor of those who are celebrating an important event, such as the birth of a baby.

This boy is planting a tree in the Jezreel Valley, one of Israel's largest tree-planting centers.

Did You Know?

Draining the swamps of the Hula Valley benefited people, but it caused trouble for the millions of birds that fly between Europe, Asia, and Africa each year. They no longer had a place to land. Israel responded by creating the Hula Nature Reserve, where flocks can land safely and feed on the local fish and insects.

The Golan Heights

The Golan Heights, captured from Syria in the 1967 Six-Day War, are at the northeastern edge of Israel. Syria maintains that the Golan Heights belong to her. Israelis remember how the Syrians on the top of the ridge bombarded Jewish settlements before the 1967 war and how the Syrians tried to recapture the Golan Heights in the 1973 Yom Kippur War.

This fertile region is dotted with many apple orchards and with vineyards that produce Israel's finest wines. In some winters, skiers can enjoy the snowy slopes of Mount Hermon, while nature lovers admire the brilliant wildflowers.

The Banyas National Park, located at the foot of Mount Hermon, is a spectacular nature preserve. Visitors can climb through Crusader ruins and explore archaeological sites, but the Banyas waterfall is the most breathtaking sight in the park. The Banyas pours into the Dan River to form the Jordan River.

The Banyas National Park may inspire you as the area's beauty inspired our ancestor who wrote: "God, I think of You in this land of the Jordan and the Hermon..." (Psalm 42:7).

The natural hot springs of Tiberias bring 140°F water up from 6,500 feet beneath the ground. Like those of the Dead Sea, these mineral-rich waters are thought to have healing powers.

Tiberias and Lake Kinneret

The Sea of Galilee, or Lake Kinneret—or **Yam Kinneret** in Hebrew—forms the eastern end of the Galilee right below the Golan Heights. On the western shore of Lake Kinneret is the city of Tiberias. Tiberias was founded in the first century CE. It became a center of Jewish learning and the residence of the Sanhedrin, the ancient Jewish high court. In the fourth century, most of what is called the Palestinian Talmud was written in Tiberias. Since then, Tiberias has been considered one of Judaism's holy cities.

Like Father, Like Son

Tiberias was founded by the son of King Herod, Herod Antipas. It was built on the remains of the biblical city of Rakkat and was named for the reigning emperor of Rome, Tiberius.

Rakkat is mentioned in the book of Joshua: "And the fortified cities were Zidim, Zeir, and Ḥammat, Rakkat, and Kinneret" (Joshua 19:35).

Archaeologists uncovered this mosaic from the third- or fourth-century synagogue in the city of Ḥammat.

Swim in Tiberias's hot springs? I don't think so! I'm not going to our Purim costume party as a boiled potato.

Map It Out

Lake Kinneret takes its name from the Hebrew word *kinor* (which originally meant "harp" but now means "violin") because the lake is shaped like a harp.

Turn to the map on page 4 and label Lake Kinneret by writing its name next to the harp.

Which river feeds into and out of Lake Kinneret?

_____

Luna Gal, on the eastern shore of Lake Kinneret, is Israel's largest water park. When I'm older, I'm going parasailing there!

I'm going too. It looks like fun!

Did You Know?

- Lake Kinneret is the only freshwater lake in Israel.

- Maimonides, the twelfth-century Jewish scholar, philosopher, and doctor—who is also known as Rambam—is buried in Tiberias.

My HEBREW DICTIONARY

מַיִם	water
הַגָּלִיל	the Galilee
יַם כִּנֶּרֶת	Lake Kinneret, Sea of Galilee
כִּנּוֹר	harp, violin

Many Israeli songs are based on verses from the Bible. The words to one song about water are from the book of Isaiah: "Therefore with joy shall you draw water from the wells of salvation" (Isaiah 12:3). The start of the chorus is easy to remember: *"Mayim, mayim, mayim, mayim."*

In Hebrew and in English, write the names of one place in Israel where you can go swimming and one place where floating is as easy as pie.

For help, check "My Hebrew Dictionary" in chapters 5 and 6.

_____

_____

_____

_____

Years ago, in kibbutz baby houses, children often were fed by kibbutz workers rather than by their parents.

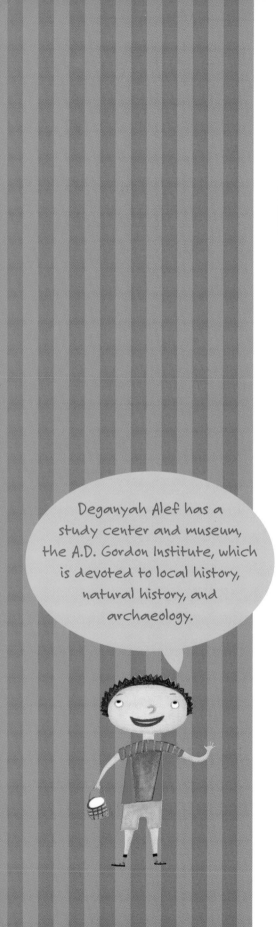

Deganyah Alef has a study center and museum, the A.D. Gordon Institute, which is devoted to local history, natural history, and archaeology.

The Growth of Kibbutzim

On the southern shore of Lake Kinneret is Deganyah Alef (which was originally called Deganyah), the first kibbutz in Israel. The kibbutz was founded in 1910 by 12 ḥalutzim from Russia who joined together to farm one plot of land.

Over time, more cooperative farms were developed throughout Israel. On each kibbutz, the people lived together and shared the work, property, and money. Everyone on the kibbutz would eat their meals together in a communal dining room, and children lived separately from their parents. Infants lived in a baby house where their parents would visit, and older children lived together in a separate building.

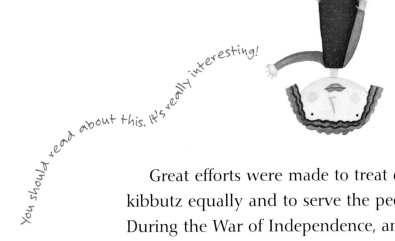

You should read about this. It's really interesting!

Great efforts were made to treat everyone on the kibbutz equally and to serve the people of Israel. During the War of Independence, and for years after, kibbutz members were considered to be among the best and bravest of soldiers, always ready to risk their lives to defend Israel's borders.

Until the late 1970s, most kibbutzim specialized in agriculture, growing crops such as oranges, grapefruits, apricots, pomegranates, dates, tomatoes, avocados, corn, and cotton, and raising poultry and livestock. As time went on, kibbutzim branched out into other areas, including manufacturing and tourism. They opened factories, hotels, museums, theaters, antique shops, amusement parks, malls, wedding halls, and restaurants on their kibbutzim, hiring people from the cities to work in them.

Fighting Pioneer Youth

Nahal, short for *Noar Halutzi Lohem,* Fighting Pioneer Youth, is a special branch of the Israeli Defense Forces. It combines military service with agricultural work on a kibbutz.

Nahal was founded to help establish new settlements in Israel, to provide security to their residents, and to teach young people agricultural skills. A number of kibbutzim were started by *Nahal* groups, and many of the *Nahal* soldiers stayed on after their army service to become permanent members of these settlements.

Rahel, a Poet of the Land

Rachel Bluwstein (1890–1931) was born in Russia, where she wrote poetry as a teenager. In 1909, the year before Deganyah was founded, she settled in *Eretz Yisrael.* She learned Hebrew and joined a farming community called Kinneret, on the shore of the lake, not far from Deganyah. There she wrote poetry under the name Rahel.

Many of Rahel's poems, including one of her most famous, *"V'ulai"* ("Perhaps"), have been set to music.

Today, there are about 270 kibbutzim in Israel. The top two kibbutz industries are tourism and plastics, and high-tech industries are on the rise. While kibbutz members still share responsibilities and help care for one another, many seek more privacy and individuality than in earlier times. For example, on most kibbutzim members no longer eat all their meals together, and children now live with their parents.

Visitors from all over the world—Sweden, Nigeria, Argentina, the United States, the Philippines, Holland, and France, Jews *and* non-Jews—live and work on kibbutzim for several weeks or months to learn about this unique way of life.

Kibbutz Ḥatzerim, near Beersheva, manufactures drip irrigation systems.

A kibbutz family relaxing with friends on Shabbat afternoon

Safed

Safed, pronounced *Tzfat* in Hebrew, is one of Israel's most beautiful towns. It stands 2,700 feet high in the hills northwest of Lake Kinneret. Safed is one of the few communities in the world where Jews have lived continuously over the centuries. Like Jerusalem and Tiberias, it is a holy place for Jews.

Many Spanish Jews settled in Safed after 1492, the year Columbus arrived in the Americas. They had been forced out of Spain because of extreme anti-Semitism. Among these new settlers were many rabbis and scholars who helped make Safed one of the world centers of Jewish learning. During this period Joseph Karo, a leading rabbi and teacher who lived in Safed, wrote the *Shulḥan Aruch*, the collection of Jewish laws that, to this day, helps guide our people.

IT'S A FACT

The first printing press in the Middle East was set up in Safed in 1563.

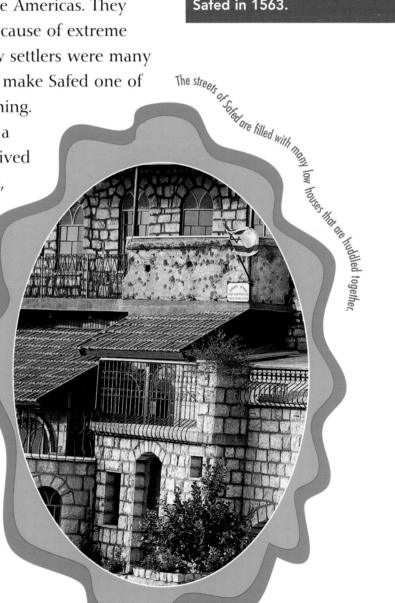

The streets of Safed are filled with many low houses that are huddled together.

Safed is now a center for Israeli art. In the town's Artists' Quarter, studios and open-air displays of painting, sculpture, and handicrafts line the steep, winding roads.

The Synagogue Quarter is known for its beautiful synagogues, many of which were built more than 400 years ago. Prayer services are still conducted in most of these synagogues.

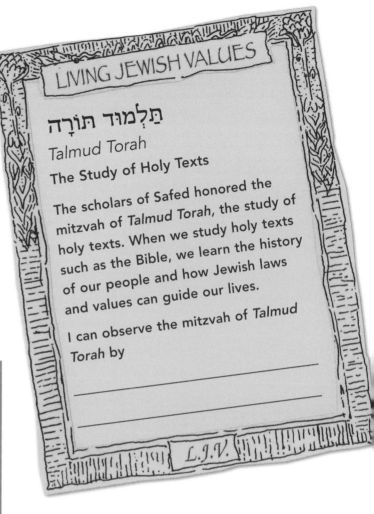

LIVING JEWISH VALUES

תַּלְמוּד תּוֹרָה

Talmud Torah
The Study of Holy Texts

The scholars of Safed honored the mitzvah of *Talmud Torah*, the study of holy texts. When we study holy texts such as the Bible, we learn the history of our people and how Jewish laws and values can guide our lives.

I can observe the mitzvah of Talmud Torah by _____

_____

_____

L.J.V.

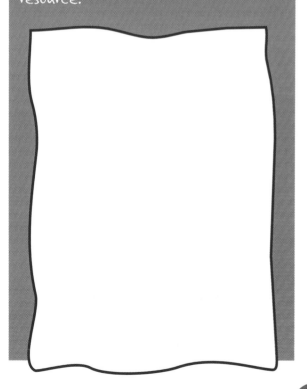

Don't Waste Water!

Israelis understand the importance of saving water. In the space below, design a poster or write a poem to remind people to conserve this natural resource.

Mountains and Valleys

From the peak of Israel's highest mountain to the bottom of its largest valley, northern Israel is a place of great natural beauty. But the area is not just a pretty landscape of fertile green hills. It also provides a crucial water supply for the rest of the country and is filled with places of historic, cultural, and religious importance to the Jewish people.

Draw here. You can draw lots of things... ↘

Greetings from Northern Israel

Send a postcard to a friend, sharing what you have learned about northern Israel. On the front of the card, draw a picture of yourself visiting the sight that is most interesting to you.

On the back of the card, tell your friend about northern Israel. Where would you like to take your friend? What part of our tour did you find most interesting? Why?

AIR MAIL

↖ Write stuff here.

7 The Kids

of Israel

I use my computer to talk to kids all around the world. I always tell them that in most ways, kids here are just like them. We like to hang out with our friends. We go to school, the movies, and the mall; we surf the Internet and listen to music. We wonder what we'll be when we grow up, and where we'll live. Our parents tell us to clean our rooms and finish our homework. Sound familiar?

But our lives are also different from those of kids in other countries. We live in the place where Judaism began, and we speak Hebrew, the language of the Bible. When we go for hikes, we walk on paths where Abraham and Sarah may have walked, and our houses are built on hills where King Solomon may have ridden his horse.

Come, let me tell you more about the kids of Israel.

Liat →

Natan

Liat's Diary

School Life

The school day starts early in Israel, at 8 A.M. Elementary students go to school until about 1 P.M., and high school students stay until about 2 P.M. Many Israeli schools have two recesses. Most children attend public schools where they study reading, writing, math, history—including world *and* Jewish history—geography, science, and Bible. Starting as early as second grade, all students study English, and some also study Arabic. By the time Israeli teens graduate from high school, many can speak three languages!

Some public schools offer additional Jewish studies. Students who attend such schools also learn Talmud and prayer. Children from Orthodox families go to religious schools called yeshivot. Girls and boys go to separate yeshivot. As part of their religious observance the boys cover their heads with kippot; the girls wear long skirts and dresses instead of pants or shorts. In the school cafeteria, the children recite both the Blessing over Bread, Hamotzi, and the Grace After Meals, Birkat Hamazon. Regular prayer services are part of the children's school day, just as they are in many Jewish day schools and yeshivot in North America.

Israeli Schools

There are seven different types of schools in Israel:

- *Mamlachti,* public secular schools with no religious studies

- *Mamlachti Dati,* public Jewish religious schools

- *Tali,* public secular schools with classes offered in Jewish studies

- *Atzma'i,* independent, ultra-Orthodox alternative schools

- *Ma'ayan Haḥinuch Hatorani,* schools for *Edot Hamizraḥ,* Easterners

- *Aravi,* Arab schools

- *Druzi,* Druze schools

ITS A FACT

- Kids in Israel go to school six days a week! The only day off Jewish students have is Saturday—Shabbat! Muslim and Druze students have Friday off, and Christian students have Sunday off.

- Students in Israel often call teachers by their first names.

Most schools in Israel are either all Jewish or all Arab. Arab and Druze children attend schools where they study their own history, religion, and culture. Their classes are taught in Arabic, although all students also learn Hebrew.

Map It Out

The village of **Neve Shalom**, or Wạhat al Salam in Arabic, was founded as a model of how Arab and Jewish families can live in harmony. For example, all the children in Neve Shalom attend the same primary schools. There are Arab as well as Jewish teachers, and the history, culture, language, and religion of both Arabs and Jews are taught.

Turn to the map on page 4 and label Neve Shalom by writing its name next to the dove. Neve Shalom lies southwest of a major city. Can you name it?

_____

What Do You Think?

The prophet Isaiah said, "My people shall dwell in an oasis of peace" (Isaiah 32:18). An oasis is a fertile spot with fresh water in the middle of a desert.

Neve Shalom means "Oasis of Peace." Do you think it is a good name for this community? Why or why not?

_____

_____

_____

_____

_____

_____

_____

רוֹדֵף שָׁלוֹם

Rodef Shalom

Seek Peace

Jewish tradition teaches that seeking peace, Rodef Shalom, is a holy act. When you help your friends settle their disagreements, or when you avoid unnecessary arguments at home, you are preparing yourself to become a peacemaker.

How else can you observe the mitzvah of Rodef Shalom?

_____

_____

_____

_____

L.J.V.

I always try to be a peacemaker with my sister Liat.

These Jerusalem high school students are e-mailing friends at Neve Shalom. They want to create a web page that will increase understanding between Arab and Jewish Israelis.

The Israeli Scouts

Israel has a variety of youth movements. Many, such as *Bnai Akiva* and *Hashomer Hatza'ir*, are based on religious and political beliefs. One youth movement that welcomes all Israeli boys and girls—religious and nonreligious, and Jews and non-Jews of all political beliefs—is the Israeli Scout Federation. The federation is connected to the international scouting movement and also to Young Judaea, an American Zionist youth movement.

Groups of Israeli Scouts spend summers working in American scout camps and Young Judaea camps.

A teenage troop of Israeli Scouts from Haifa

Popular after-school group activities include soccer, karate, dance, and ceramics. These activities are called *hugim,* or clubs. Of course, a favorite, *unofficial* after-school activity is hanging out with your *hevrah* or circle of friends.

The scouts, or **tzofim,** wear colorful neckerchiefs and khaki uniforms that are similar to those worn by scouts in the United States. Unlike scouts in the United States, Israeli boys and girls belong to the same scout troops. *Tzofim* meet after school and on weekends. They hike, do volunteer work, visit museums, and go on overnight trips. Sitting around the campfire, they discuss everything from current events to their favorite TV shows.

My HEBREW DICTIONARY

חֶבְרָה	circle of friends
צוֹפִים	scouts
נְוֵה שָׁלוֹם	Neve Shalom, Oasis of Peace

Hevrah comes from the same root as *haver* (male) and *haverah* (female), which mean "friend." *Haver* and *haverah* also mean "member." For example, a member of the Knesset is called a *haver* or *haverat Knesset.*

In high school, many *tzofim* join the *Gadna*, the youth corps of the Israeli armed forces. (*Gadna* is short for *Gedudei Noar*, "Youth Battalions.") In the *Gadna*, young men and women learn about their responsibility to defend their country. Some teenagers volunteer as *madrichim*, or leaders, for the younger children in the *tzofim*.

Entertainment and Sports

Israeli kids enjoy spending time with their *ḥevrah* and watching television, just like kids all around the world. They also enjoy attending soccer and basketball games, going to movies and concerts, and listening to CDs.

In hot weather, Israeli kids head straight for the mayim, or water.

Israeli kids listen to music from Europe, North America, South America, Africa, and Asia, in styles ranging from classical to folk to pop to hip-hop and rock. They also enjoy the music of Israeli singers, songwriters, and musicians. One of the most popular is Noa, an Israeli-born, American-raised daughter of Yemenite parents. Noa, who spent much of her childhood in New York City, began writing songs at the age of eight. Her unique mixture of Israeli-American music has attracted fans in Japan, France, Italy, Spain, the Netherlands, and other countries around the world.

You'll be surprised how easy it can be to jump right into Israeli life.

Sheshbesh, or backgammon, is a popular board game in Israel.

Whether it's the latest Israeli or Hollywood film, Israeli kids can see it at their local multiplex theater. Of course, they sit back and enjoy it in Hebrew!

My favorite basketball team is Maccabi Tel Aviv! As soon as I learn to dunk, I'm trying out for the team!

Israeli kids participate in many of the same sports that you do. They bike, play tennis, water-ski, and skate. There is not much baseball or football to be found in Israel, but almost every Israeli child learns to play soccer and basketball—the most popular team sports in Israel. Most cities have professional basketball and soccer teams.

Every four years, Israel hosts the Maccabiah Games. Jewish athletes from around the world participate in these "Jewish Olympics" at the Ramat Gan Stadium outside Tel Aviv.

No matter what sports you like, in Israel you are likely to find friends who share your interests.

Sports Heroes

Yael Arad at the 1992 Olympics

Tal Brody (1943–) was born in Trenton, New Jersey, and was offered the chance to play professional basketball for the Baltimore Bullets in 1965. Instead, he led the U.S. team to the gold medal in the Maccabiah Games. It was his first visit to Israel, but he didn't want to leave. Tal returned to live in Israel in 1970, joining the Maccabi Tel Aviv team. He introduced Israeli children to basketball through his after-school program, "Let's Play Ball!"

In 1979, two years before he retired from professional basketball, the State of Israel awarded Tal its highest honor, the Israel Prize, for his contribution to sports and education in Israel.

Yael Arad (1967–) competed in the 1992 Olympic Games in Barcelona. The silver medal she earned in the judo competition was Israel's first-ever Olympic prize! Now back home in Israel, Yael teaches judo to kids.

Keren Leibowitch (1973–), who lost the use of her legs as a result of an injury she suffered in the army, is a world-class swimmer. In 1997, at the European championships for athletes with disabilities, Keren won a gold medal in the 100-meter backstroke and three silver medals. She holds the world record for both the 50-meter freestyle and the 100-meter backstroke.

I'm athletic too!

When the first Maccabiah Games were held in 1932, 390 athletes from 14 countries took part. Forty-five years later, the 1997 games welcomed over 5,500 Jewish athletes from more than 50 countries. Many famous athletes have performed in the Maccabiah Games. The American swimmer Mark Spitz competed in 1969. Just a few years later, in 1972, he went on to win a record 7 gold medals for the United States in the international Olympic Games.

IT'S A FACT

Basketball was played in the Maccabiah Games before it was ever played in the Olympics.

Did You Know?

Although there is no professional baseball played in Israel, some North Americans who made *aliyah* have organized a Little League. They also run a baseball summer camp for Israeli children.

Favorite Foods

Because Israel is a melting pot for so many different cultures, its menu choices represent styles and tastes from all over the globe. Traditional Middle Eastern food, such as ḥummus, is sold next to spicy Yemenite dishes and the sweet cheese blintzes of Eastern Europe.

Israelis shop for food in supermarkets and in open-air markets.

If Israel had a national food, it would be falafel, which is chickpea balls fried in oil. You can grab a falafel-stuffed pita almost anywhere—at a restaurant, at a *shuk*, or from a street vendor, and you can pile on all the toppings you like—sauerkraut, salad, pickles, French fries, teḥina (sesame sauce), and *ḥarif* (hot sauce). Of course, Israeli kids also like a lot of *your* favorite foods. They each have a favorite pizza parlor and love to finish a meal with a double scoop of ice cream.

Sufganiyot, or jelly doughnuts, are popular Ḥanukkah treats. Fried in oil, they are a delicious way to celebrate the Festival of Lights. And besides hamburgers and hot dogs, Israelis grill *shishlik* and *kebab* on backyard barbecues.

Do your parents remind you to eat your vegetables? Israeli parents give this instruction at every meal—even at the breakfast table! A typical Israeli breakfast can include a pile of chopped tomatoes, cucumbers, and peppers, topped with olives and cheese.

Israeli bagels may look and taste a little different from the ones you're used to, but one thing's for sure—they're "hole-y."

Israeli kids love to eat ice-cream cones, sandwiches, and sundaes, but they call ice cream *glidah*. Can you find the Hebrew word for ice cream in the picture?

Don't forget about me when you buy treats!

After school, I like to dip a pita bread into hummus, a spread made of ground chick-peas and olive oil. I top it off with a dash of za'atar, a mix-ture of Middle Eastern spices and herbs.

For a special treat while visiting the Neot Kedumim Biblical Nature Reserve near Jerusalem, you can make pita the old-fashioned way.

Proud to Be an Israeli Kid

In many ways, Israeli kids are like kids from any-where else. They go to school, look forward to holi-days, and have favorite hobbies like computers, art, and soccer. But an Israeli childhood is also unique, because it is spent in the homeland of the Jewish people—celebrating Jewish holidays as national holidays, e-mailing friends in Hebrew, and studying the Bible in public school.

Tell your friends at home about growing up in Israel.

Shalom,

Israeli kids go to school _____ days a week. They not only study the same subjects we do, they also study _____ and_____ _____. In the village of _____, Arab and Jewish children attend the same school and learn about each other's history, culture, and religion.

Israeli kids have a scout program called the _____. Like us, Israeli kids love sports, especially _____ and _____. The _____ _____, or "Jewish Olympics," are held in Israel every four years.

Israelis call their circle of friends their _____.

L'hitra'ot! See you soon!

8 Peace
and Security

Shalom! My name is Yael. I'm Liat's next-door neighbor. My father is a colonel in the Israeli Defense Forces. I am proud of him because he works to keep Israel safe and secure. But I worry that he may be hurt if there is a terrorist attack or if there is another war. I hope that such things never happen again, not here or in any other country.

Come, let me tell you about the Israeli Defense Forces and Israel's relationship with the Arab nations since the State of Israel was established. In the past there have been many wars, but we hope that some day soon there will be shalom.

Yael

Yael's father

Serving in the Israeli Armed Forces

For nearly 2,000 years, the Jewish people had no army of its own. Then, the *Haganah* was created to protect the Jewish settlers of Palestine. The *Haganah*, or Defense, was small and poorly armed, but it was able to win the War of Independence in 1948. Today, Israel's army is known as **Tz'va Haganah Leyisrael**, the Israeli Defense Forces—*Tzahal*, or IDF for short.

In many countries, citizens may choose to join the armed forces. In Israel, most Israeli teens are drafted into the armed forces at age 18. Boys serve for 3 years, while girls serve for 20 months.

The IDF is made up of several different corps, including the army, navy, and air force. There are many highly specialized jobs to be filled in the IDF. A soldier might drive a tank, parachute from a plane, train other soldiers to use sophisticated electronic equipment, fly a helicopter, navigate a submarine, or serve in the military police. There are also computer programmers, medics, teachers, translators, rabbis, cooks, and photographers in the IDF.

Israeli teens also get the right to vote when they are 18.

Members of the *Haganah* defending Jewish settlements in 1947

IDF to the Rescue

The IDF not only defends Israel, it also helps people from other countries. For example, in 1999, when Turkey suffered an earthquake that killed and injured thousands of people, the IDF sent a 200-member team and a field hospital to help in the rescue effort. Two Turkish families were so grateful that one named its newborn son Israel and the other named its newborn daughter Ziona.

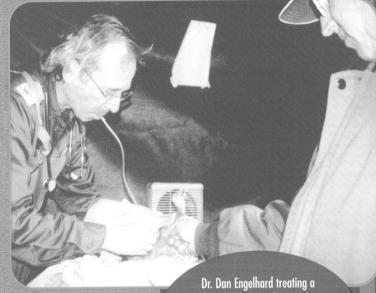

Dr. Dan Engelhard treating a newborn baby in a refugee camp in Kosovo. Dr. Engelhard was part of the IDF medical rescue mission to the war-torn Balkans during the spring of 1999.

This makes me feel so proud of Israel.

The Reserves

After completing their required military service, Israeli men and women join the reserves, or *milu'im*. They leave their jobs and their families for about four weeks each year to train and practice their military skills, because reservists can be called into service in the event of a war. Women with no children serve in the reserves until age 34. Men serve until age 55.

After the American embassies in Kenya and Tanzania were bombed by terrorists in 1998, the Israeli Defense Forces sent 150 soldiers, doctors, and rescue specialists to help the victims. In response, U.S. congressman Charles Rangel said, "The Israeli people played an extraordinary role in the search and rescue efforts....The American people are very grateful for such generous and unselfish assistance."

My HEBREW DICTIONARY

צְבָא הַגַנָּה לְיִשְׂרָאֵל   Israeli Defense Forces

מְלוּאִים   military reserve duty

The first word of the term Magen David, or Shield of David, comes from the same root as *Haganah*, meaning to "protect" or "defend."

The tradition of defending Israel is passed on from one generation to the next. These children will join the IDF when they are 18 years old.

Who Is Not Required to Serve?

Although almost every Israeli must serve in the armed forces, there are some exceptions. Most ultra-Orthodox men do not serve. Some modern Orthodox women serve in the IDF. Other Orthodox women who want to serve their country may choose to spend 2 years in the National Service, where they volunteer in hospitals, teach Hebrew to new immigrants, or work as guides at nature reserves.

Israel's Arab citizens are not obligated to serve in the IDF, although some volunteer to do so. Because Israeli Arabs may have family and friends serving in the armies of neighboring Arab countries, Israel does not demand that its Arab citizens be willing to serve in the IDF. Most of the Arabs who volunteer are Bedouin.

The Glue that Holds Israel Together

Service in the IDF is an important experience that is shared by almost all of Israel's young men and women. While learning useful skills, they also meet people from all over the country and from backgrounds different from their own. Some people say that the army is the glue that holds Israel together. Because most Israelis have served in the army, they come to feel connected to one another, to the land, and to the history of our people.

Ayala Marari, a second lieutenant in the Israeli Air Force, is a graduate of the Technion's Aeronautical Engineering Department. She is one of many Technion graduates who have helped build and maintain Israel's technological supremacy.

Did you ever hear of a general who is a mother of three, keeps a kosher house, and rushes home each week to observe Shabbat? That's General Dotan!

Did You Know?

In 1984, Amira Dotan became the head of *Chen*, the women's division of the IDF. Dotan was the first woman to rise to the rank of brigadier general.

General Dotan was eager to help women achieve important positions in the army by guiding them into the fields of electronics and technology. But, at the time, most girls were not encouraged to study these subjects in school. General Dotan traveled to schools throughout Israel to deliver her message. Because of her efforts, there are now many women who have the training and skills to use sophisticated equipment and computers to defend Israel.

Make a Care Package

Soldiers sometimes receive care packages from civilians who want to show their appreciation. Often, a whole town will "adopt" a military unit and send its soldiers gifts for Rosh Hashanah or Passover. Draw the things you would want to send to a soldier who was far from home, protecting Israel. Label each item and explain why you would send it.

Israel's War of Independence

As soon as the State of Israel was established on May 14, 1948, Israel's Arab neighbors attacked, and the Israeli War of Independence began. By the time it ended eight months later, more than 6,000 Jews had been killed and approximately half a million Palestinian Arabs had become refugees in Arab countries. The war was over, but no peace treaty had been signed, and hundreds of thousands of Palestinian Arab refugees believed their homeland had been unjustly taken from them.

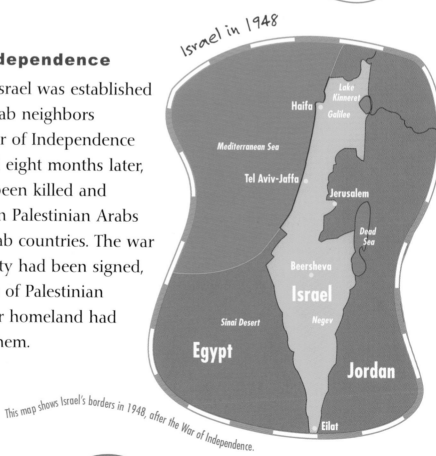

Israel in 1948

This map shows Israel's borders in 1948, after the War of Independence.

To guard against attacks by Arabs, Jewish policemen in the Tel Aviv-Jaffa area built defense posts out of oil drums, barrels, and the pointed tops of metal gates.

An American Hero

Soon after the War of Independence began, the Arabs cut the only through-road from Tel Aviv to Jerusalem. The 50,000 Jewish inhabitants of Jerusalem were cut off from their supply route, without food and ammunition.

A small Piper Cub plane made two trips a day. In the morning it carried a barrel of flour in the passenger's seat; in the afternoon, a barrel filled with ammunition. But this was scarcely enough. Convoys of armored vehicles—trucks with iron plates fastened over their windows—tried to make their way through, but the Arabs destroyed almost every truck that tried. You can still see the shattered trucks lining the road to Jerusalem when you enter Sha'ar Hagai, the Gate to the Valley.

To the rescue came a Jewish-American graduate of West Point, Colonel David Marcus, a veteran of the U.S. army. He surveyed the maps and discovered a few tiny paths paralleling the major road. He was assigned men who labored day and night to make these paths into a road—known as the "Burma Road"—passable by light trucks and even herds of cows.

Jerusalem was saved!

During the war, Colonel Marcus was given the undercover name "Mickey Stone" to hide his identity. In 1966, Hollywood made a movie, *Cast a Giant Shadow*, of this extraordinary mission. The Jewish-American actor Kirk Douglas played the role of Colonel Marcus.

This tank was left on the road to Jerusalem as a memorial to the soldiers who lost their lives bringing supplies to the city during Israel's War of Independence.

LIVING JEWISH VALUES

פִּדְיוֹן שְׁבוּיִים

Pidyon Shevuyim

Freeing of Jewish Captives

Pidyon Shevuyim is the mitzvah of rescuing Jewish captives. It teaches us to take responsibility for such Jews by helping to free them. Despite the danger in trying to enter Jerusalem during the War of Independence, there were people who risked their lives to help Jews caught inside the city without food or medicine.

Operation Moses, the airlift of Ethiopian Jews discussed in chapter 2, is another example of Pidyon Shevuyim.

Explain the mitzvah of Pidyon Shevuyim in your own words.

_____

_____

L.J.V.

Israel also played an important role in freeing Jewish captives in Yemen and the former Soviet Union.

The Suez War

There were no wars for several years, but there were many acts of Arab terrorism that killed or injured hundreds of Israeli citizens. Then, in 1956, Egypt blocked the Strait of Tiran in the Gulf of Akaba (the Arab name for the Gulf of Eilat) near the southern tip of Israel, cutting off Israel from Africa and Asia. In addition, Israel feared that Egypt (which had been newly supplied with weapons from the Soviet Union) was planning an attack. Israel decided to strike first. And so began the Suez War, also called the Sinai Campaign, on October 29. The war lasted eight days. Israel agreed to return the Sinai Desert and the Gaza Strip, which it had captured. But like the War of Independence, the Sinai Campaign ended without a peace treaty.

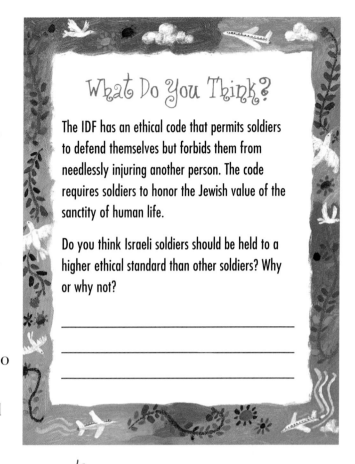

What Do You Think?

The IDF has an ethical code that permits soldiers to defend themselves but forbids them from needlessly injuring another person. The code requires soldiers to honor the Jewish value of the sanctity of human life.

Do you think Israeli soldiers should be held to a higher ethical standard than other soldiers? Why or why not?

_____

_____

_____

I love to read maps.

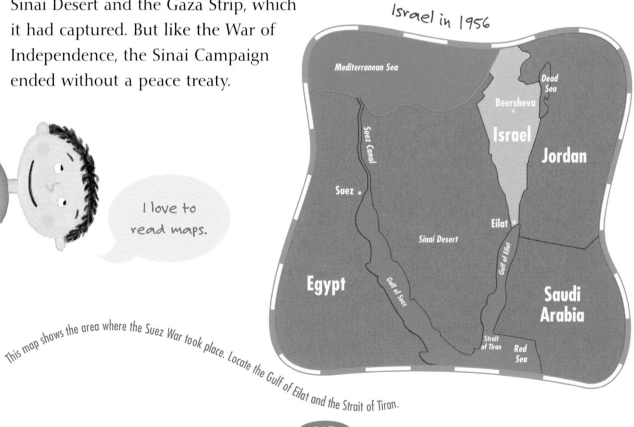

Israel in 1956

This map shows the area where the Suez War took place. Locate the Gulf of Eilat and the Strait of Tiran.

The Six-Day War

Arab terrorist raids began again in 1965, and in 1967 Syria, Egypt, and Jordan prepared for war. For a second time, Egypt blockaded the Gulf of Akaba, cutting off Israel's oil supply. On June 5, Israel again struck first. In six days the war was over. Israel had gained control of the West Bank of Jordan and the Golan Heights of Syria, and had regained the Sinai Desert and Gaza Strip. But most importantly, it now had control of East Jerusalem, including the Old City! Jerusalem was united, and once again Jews could pray at the *Kotel*.

Israeli troops celebrating their astonishing victory in the Six-Day War

Israel After the Six-Day War

- Lebanon
- Golan Heights
- Haifa
- Tiberias
- Syria
- Territories Israel gained in the Six-Day War
- Tel Aviv-Jaffa
- West Bank
- Mediterranean Sea
- Jerusalem
- Gaza Strip
- Israel
- Jordan
- Sinai Desert
- Eilat
- Egypt
- Saudi Arabia

All around the world, Jews and many non-Jews celebrated Israel's victory in the Six-Day War. Like the story of David and Goliath, the small nation of Israel had defeated its powerful foes. Throughout Israel, there was dancing in the streets. For the first time, Israelis began to feel more secure about their future.

But, as a result of the war, Israel also found itself governing 1 million Arabs who lived in the newly conquered territories. The Israelis felt very powerful ruling the Palestinians; the Palestinians felt oppressed and became determined to become an independent people with their own state.

The Yom Kippur War

On Yom Kippur in 1973, Israel was caught off guard. While many Israelis were in synagogue, praying and fasting on this, the holiest day of the Jewish year, Egypt and Syria attacked. The IDF immediately called up its reservists, but it was almost impossible to react quickly enough.

The outnumbered Israeli soldiers heroically stopped the Syrians' invasion of the Golan Heights, but the Syrians broke through Israeli border defenses, killing hundreds of Israelis. The Syrians stopped their attack and the IDF, mobilizing its reserve units, conquered additional land in Syria.

You can read about David and Goliath in the Bible, in the book of Samuel. The story tells how, before David was king of Israel, he fought and killed the giant Goliath with just a slingshot. Why do you think people sometimes compare Israel to David?

_____

_____

_____

_____

My mom grew up in Cape Town, South Africa. She told me that when Israel's victory in the Six-Day War was announced, her school—Weizmann Primary School—cancelled all classes for the day. The students gathered in the school's courtyard and danced Israeli dances for hours. Many parents joined the celebration and cried with joy as they watched their children dance.

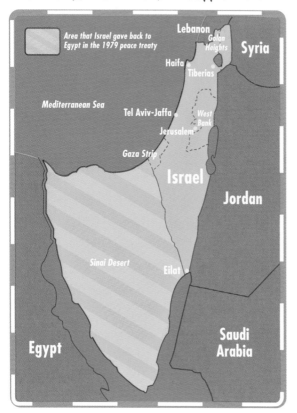

The situation in the Sinai was worse for the Israelis. The Egyptian forces were protected with land-to-air missiles that severely reduced the effectiveness of the Israeli air support. On the southern border, 436 Israelis in bunkers faced 600,000 Egyptian soldiers!

Despite great difficulty and the loss of many lives, and with extensive supplies of military equipment from the United States, Israel managed to turn the tide. As Israeli troops neared Cairo, the capital of Egypt, a truce was put into effect. This led, under U.S. mediation, to the Camp David Accords (1978) and to the signing of a peace treaty between Israel and Egypt, the first peace treaty between Israel and any of its Arab neighbors.

Throughout Israel there are signs that say miklat, or "shelter." They point to shelters where civilians can find protection in the event of attacks or war.

Israel After the Yom Kippur War

Area that Israel gave back to Egypt in the 1979 peace treaty

Lebanon
Golan Heights
Syria
Haifa
Tiberias
Mediterranean Sea
Tel Aviv-Jaffa
West Bank
Jerusalem
Gaza Strip
Israel
Jordan
Sinai Desert
Eilat
Egypt
Saudi Arabia

Which desert area was given back to Egypt in the 1979 peace treaty?

The Israel Air Force Museum is located near Beersheva. It has over 90 airplanes, including Israel's first fighter plane, the Kfir. Like many Israeli kids, I am both proud of our air force and I pray for a time when its planes are used only for peaceful purposes.

A First Peace Treaty Is Signed

On March 26, 1979, with the help of American president Jimmy Carter, Israeli prime minister Menaḥem Begin and Egyptian president Anwar Sadat signed a peace treaty. Based on that treaty, Israel gave back the entire Sinai Desert in return for peace with Egypt.

From left to right, Anwar Sadat, Jimmy Carter, and Menaḥem Begin after signing the Israeli-Egyptian peace treaty in March 1979

Egypt and Israel hoped that other Arab countries would want to make peace, too, but instead they were angry with Egypt. The Palestine Liberation Organization, or PLO, which was the leading representative of the Palestinian people, refused to participate in peace talks, and, from its bases in Lebanon (Israel's northern neighbor), the PLO engaged in terrorist attacks on Israel.

Did You Know?

In 1978, Menaḥem Begin and Anwar Sadat were awarded the Nobel Prize for Peace for their efforts to end the Israeli-Arab conflict.

The War in Lebanon

In June 1982, Israel sent soldiers into Lebanon because of the growing number of PLO bases in southern Lebanon. The IDF forced the PLO to leave Beirut, the capital, as well as southern Lebanon. Israel stayed on the outskirts of Beirut to prevent the PLO's return. But many Israelis felt that this military operation had gone on for too long, without enough reason. By early 1985, the IDF units had withdrawn from most of Lebanon, leaving only a small strip of southern Lebanon under Israeli control.

Israel and Her Northern Neighbors

Yasir Arafat, chairman of the Palestine Liberation Organization, wearing a kaffiyeh, a traditional headcovering worn by Arab men

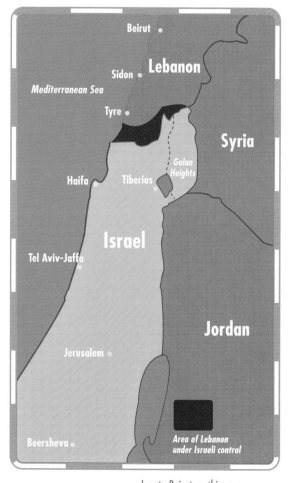

Area of Lebanon under Israeli control

Locate Beirut on this map.

Israeli troops leaving Lebanon

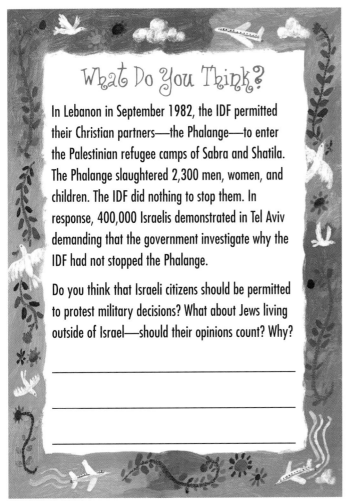

What Do You Think?

In Lebanon in September 1982, the IDF permitted their Christian partners—the Phalange—to enter the Palestinian refugee camps of Sabra and Shatila. The Phalange slaughtered 2,300 men, women, and children. The IDF did nothing to stop them. In response, 400,000 Israelis demonstrated in Tel Aviv demanding that the government investigate why the IDF had not stopped the Phalange.

Do you think that Israeli citizens should be permitted to protest military decisions? What about Jews living outside of Israel—should their opinions count? Why?

_____

_____

_____

The Intifada

In late 1987, the *Intifada*, meaning "shaking off" or "uprising" in Arabic, broke out in the Gaza Strip and in Arab towns and villages on the West Bank. The Palestinians living in these areas rebelled against Israeli control, rioting in the streets. Children threw stones at Israeli soldiers, and Israeli soldiers responded with tear gas and rubber and plastic bullets. Some soldiers panicked, shooting and killing civilians.

In September 1991, the Israeli army announced that since the beginning of the Intifada, 1,225 Arabs and 13 Israeli soldiers had been killed. People in Israel and around the world wanted the fighting to stop.

A Second Peace Treaty Is Signed

Finally, in 1993, with the help of the U.S. government, a peace arrangement called the Declaration of Principles was signed by PLO chairman Yasir Arafat and Israeli prime minister Yitzhak Rabin. It was signed at the White House in Washington, D.C., using the very same table on which Menahem Begin and Anwar Sadat had signed the Camp David Accords in 1978. Yasir Arafat, on behalf of the Palestinian people, recognized the State of Israel and rejected the use of violence toward its citizens. In return, Israel agreed to give partial independence to the Gaza Strip and parts of the West Bank, and to come to final agreement on the other issues—including control over Jerusalem—at a later time.

In his speech, Yitzhak Rabin addressed the Palestinian people, "We say to you today in a loud and clear voice: Enough of blood and tears. Enough. We harbor no hatred toward you. We have no desire for revenge. We, like you, are people who want to build a home, plant a tree, love, live side by side with you."

A Vision of Peace

The prophet Isaiah had a beautiful vision of a time when there would be no more wars. He wrote, "And they shall beat their swords into plowshares, and their spears into pruning hooks; nation shall not lift up sword against nation, neither shall they learn war any more" (Isaiah 2:4).

This verse from the book of Isaiah is inscribed on a monument across the street from the United Nations in New York City.

In 1994, the Nobel Prize for Peace was jointly awarded to Yitzhak Rabin, Shimon Peres (a former Israeli prime minister), and Yasir Arafat for their roles in helping to bring peace to the Middle East.

On October 26, 1994, Jordan's King Hussein signed a peace treaty with Israel in which the two governments agreed on the borders between their countries and on how to share the precious waters of the Yarmuk and Jordan Rivers, and the water of the Arava.

Yitzhak Rabin (1922–1995) was a military commander who served in the defense of Israel for 27 years and then became prime minister. He heeded the words of Isaiah when he signed the peace treaty and said, "Let us pray that a day will come when we all will say: Farewell to arms."

An Israeli soldier (right) and Jordanian soldier (left) look forward to a future of peace and friendship.

A Fallen Soldier of Peace

On November 4, 1995, a rally was held in Tel Aviv in support of the peace process. As the rally came to an end, from a high platform, Yitzhak Rabin joined the crowd in singing "The Song of Peace":

So sing only a song for peace
Do not whisper a prayer
Better sing a song for peace
With a great shout.

When the song ended, Rabin left the platform. As he went toward his car he was shot and killed by Yigal Amir, a Jewish religious fanatic who opposed the peace process.

At Yitzhak Rabin's funeral President and Mrs. Clinton (first row) were among those who offered the Rabin family and all Israel their sympathy and hopes for shalom.

Looking Forward to a Better Future

So far, the road to peace has been long and rocky. Slowly, though, progress has been made. Like people all around the world, Israelis want peace. They also want to be safe—free from attacks by terrorists and foreign soldiers. Finding and following the path toward peace and security is the greatest challenge of our time—for Israel and for all nations.

Best Wishes for Peace

Send a postcard to the prime minister of Israel, an Arab leader, or the president of the United States. On the front of the card, draw a picture of what you think Israel will look like when there is peace with all its Arab neighbors.

On the back of the card, share your thoughts about Israel's struggle for peace and what your hopes are for the future.

AIR MAIL

↖ Write stuff here.

9 The Hope
and the Promise

Thank you for joining our tour of Israel's historical and holy places, as well as the exciting cities of our modern state.

Through the centuries, there have been many other nations who, like the Jews, have been exiled, or forced to leave their homelands. But in time, each ceased being a people, for without a country they had no reason to stay together. We are the only exiled nation that remained one people, even though we had to wait almost 2,000 years to return to our homeland.

The modern State of Israel breathed new life into the Jewish people. It restored our pride and our strength as schools, libraries, synagogues, hospitals, and museums were built, and the desert bloomed.

As we look into the future, we are hopeful that peace will come to Israel and that, in partnership with Jews around the world, Israel will remain strong and fulfill its promise as the homeland of the Jewish people.

Please be in touch and visit us often. Israel is our home and yours!